180: STORIES OF PEOPLE WHO CHANGED
THEIR LIVES BY CHANGING THEIR MINDS

Copyright 2010
by The House Studio

ISBN 978-0-8341-2512-4

Printed in the United States of America

Cover & Interior Design by SharpSeven Design

10 9 8 7 6 5 4 3 2 1

INTRODUCTION

Whenever a politician or leader changes her mind about something, critics are quick to pounce: she waffled; she's putting her finger to the wind and is only pandering to public opinion; she flip-flopped.

Whenever a politician or leader holds fast to a position or opinion, critics are quick to pounce: he's bullheaded, stubborn; he refuses to believe the facts; he's blindly supporting the party line.

Somewhere between those two extremes are ordinary people like us who want to be viewed as neither wafflers nor stubborn. We think we know what we believe and think about things, but every now and then those beliefs and opinions are challenged. We try to be open-minded without automatically accepting every new idea that comes along. Some topics almost beg for a regular change.

For example, how have you changed your mind over the years on these important questions:

What's the best movie you've ever seen?

What's your favorite band?

Who's the all-time best athlete in the world?

Who's more obnoxious—Simon Cowell or Perez Hilton?

Mac or PC?

Differences in personal preferences about music or movies (or sports teams or ice-cream flavors or computers) make great conversation over coffee, but a new band comes along and you have a new favorite. For the most part, we find it easy to change our minds about these sorts of things. The stakes seem to get higher as the topics become more serious:

Should gays be given the right to marry?

If you oppose abortion, should you also oppose capital punishment?

Is it ever right to torture captured terrorists?

Will a devout follower of Islam go to heaven?

Regardless of how *you* would answer any of the above, can you imagine your views changing over time?

The purpose of this book is not to get you to change your mind about anything. At the risk of sounding arrogant, we're pretty sure you will. We asked people from all walks of life to contribute essays on how they have changed their minds on something. Interestingly, not one person said they have never changed their mind. Some of you who consider yourselves Republicans will become Democrats someday. Some of you who are opposed to war will become more hawkish than Dick Cheney. Some of you who wear boxers will switch to briefs, and we don't want to hear about it!

What we hope this book does for you is help you better understand that the process of changing your mind is as important as the change itself; and that the process for one person may not necessarily be the process another uses. As you will discover from their stories, these writers didn't just one day decide to change their minds. It was a process, sometimes taking months—even years. They confronted new facts and had to decide what to do with them. They sought the counsel of others—usually from people who were older. They searched the Scriptures. They prayed. They listened.

Even though we're not out to change your mind on anything, we hope to stretch it a little. The views expressed in these chapters may conflict with what you believe. Some conflict with what we believe. *Newsweek* religion reporter Lisa Miller once wrote, "What's dangerous about the world today is not belief in God, or unbelief, but ruthless certainty." We're pretty certain about a lot of things, but we hope we are never so certain that we become arrogant and dismissive of others. If you are quite certain that women should have the right to an abortion, let Frederica Mathewes-Green's essay on page 53 test your ruthless certainty. If you think global warming and other environmental issues are overstated by liberal tree-huggers, wrestle with Nancy Sleeth's essay on page 65. If you think Christian movies do more harm than good, check out Rich Peluso's essay on page 43. In fact, check them all out. We tackle everything from *Is the Bible true?* to *Should Christians trick-or-treat?* to the role of nail polish in spiritual growth.

By the way. What *is* the best movie you've ever seen?

-the House Studio staff

TABLE OF CONTENTS

LIVING THE ADVENTURE
SCOTT BOLINDER

What is a social worker doing in publishing? I've often been asked that question over the past thirty years, since my professional training and most advanced degree is a master's in social work. I even practiced for four years as an officer in the army, fulfilling an ROTC obligation. Truth is, a bigger principle has influenced me starting early in life: I was always the kid who liked to change the furniture in my bedroom just for the sake of change. This has not only helped me face change with ease but many times has led me to seek change.

After graduating from college with a degree in English literature, I went immediately to graduate school in social work. From there I entered the army and spent four years working as a clinical social worker in a mechanized infantry unit and then in a base hospital. I liked the work—really—but this was during the time just following the Vietnam War in the mid-70s, and as I used to say, "I got ten years of experience in four actual years."

I suppose I was somewhat burned out by the end of my military commitment, but somehow I felt that continuing in my field was not the right next step in my adventure. To be sure, the nor-

mal step would have been for me to move into the private practice offer that was waiting for me in Colorado where we were
living, then with our first child. But my wife and I said from the
day we were married that we wanted to "live the adventure"
God has in store for us. So we essentially took out a blank sheet
of paper and began to write a new chapter for our lives.

Based on having been dealt good hands in our upbringings,
we thought God's plan for us would land us in an exciting "salt
and light" role in the business world where we could demon-
strate what healthy Christianity looks like. So I sent resumés
to multiple companies, seeking a job in sales, not the more expected field of human resources, given my background in social work. We were seeking adventure, after all. Soon I was im-
mersed in a serious escapade as a sales representative selling
advertising for a brand new business magazine in the design en-
gineering field. My plan was taking shape, and we were feeling
pretty good about orchestrating this change that would allow us
to live our adventure.

Then God, in his mercy, reminded us that while he loves
our sense of spontaneity, he really prefers to orchestrate things
overall. In fact, Proverbs 16:9 describes this polarity well: "In
his heart, a man plans his course, but the LORD determines his
steps." What a wonderful mix of mystery and confidence. After
almost a year to the date of starting my job in advertising sales,
I was approached by a good friend who asked me to come work
with him at a ministry that published a youth magazine called
Campus Life. That invitation ended up leading to a decision that
was not only a defining moment in our story but one of our first

real opportunities to discern God's will regarding a "big decision."

Remember, we had said from the outset that we wanted to live the adventure God had in store for us. But when the time came to really be serious about that, it required the hard work of making pros and cons lists, seeking the counsel of trusted friends, listening carefully to the promptings of God's spirit, and finally discerning what we felt was God's assignment.

On paper it did not make sense to switch jobs like this. But in the end, we embraced the fact that, as theologian Robert Webber put it, "God owns the narrative." We changed direction and took the plunge! Thirty years later, we still look back on that decision as a major change in the trajectory of our lives. Indeed, as the old chorus says so well, "The Lord knows the way through the wilderness; all you gotta do is follow...."

Scott Bolinder has enjoyed a distinguished career in publishing. As a vice president at CTi, he served as publisher of **Campus Life** *and* **Marriage Partnership** *magazines. At Zondervan, he led the book and Bible divisions as publisher and currently is president of global publishing at Biblica (formerly the International Bible Society).*

My mama took her role as an army wife so seriously that her catty friends began to refer to her as "the General." Suffice it to say, Mama did not believe in coddling children, especially not whiny children. Life with Mama was its own form of boot camp.

My earliest childhood memory is all convoluted because I still can't figure out what scared me more: the thunderstorm outside or my mama's rebuke.

It was a spring morning in 1960, and we were living in a matchbox brick home next to the baseball park just off Morris Road in Columbus, Georgia. Daddy headed off to work at Fort Benning before I even crawled out of bed. Brother John was up the road, squirming in a desk at Edgewood Elementary, and Mama was in the back room, tending to my baby sister.

My three-year-old self, dressed in a white cotton slip, stood at the sliding glass door that led out to the backyard. I had to reach up to grab the handle to slide the door open, not that I had any intentions of doing so. A hard rain was flooding the sandbox. The tops of the pine trees were bowing like minions in the presence of English royalty. A thunderous hand hurled pinecones toward the house, rattling the wood floors beneath my bare feet. I pressed my nose up against the glass door and hollered for Mama.

"What is the matter?" Mama asked irritably as she walked into the room.

"That!" I said, pointing at the dark sky and continuing to cry. "I'm scared!"

Mama rolled her almond eyes and sternly said, "Well if it scares you, get away from the door, silly."

Oh.

It hadn't occurred to me to move away from terror.

———————————

My fascination with the fearful things of life has not abated one bit. I grew up to become a crime reporter. There are times when I can still be found with my nose pressed up against the glass, scared and wailing.

During one recent crying jag, my youngest daughter, who works in the medical field, asked tentatively, "Are you having a mental breakdown, Mama?"

"No," I replied, crying still. "If I'm having a breakdown, it's a nervous breakdown, not a mental one."

"What are you scared of?" my daughter asked.

"Nothing," I said.

It was a lie.

I should have told her the truth. I should have told her that if life doesn't scare you, you're probably dead already.

I should have answered, "Everything."

The experts who study these matters say it is our relationships with our fathers that shape our images of God. If that's true, it certainly helps explain why for much of my life I figured God for the guy who goes AWOL at the first sign of trouble.

Daddy was killed in Vietnam just six short years after I stood at the back door of that brick house watching that terrifying storm roll in. It makes me sad to talk about all that, so if you want to know more about that, you can read the book I wrote about it: *After the Flag Has Been Folded* (Wm. Morrow, 2006).

For many years after my father died, I felt like he'd abandoned our family. I felt the sorrow and anger of his leaving as surely as if he'd run off with some boozy blonde woman.

Mama had bad dreams that Daddy had done just that, gone off to live with some other family, to make love to some other woman.

We didn't talk about how we were feeling. We just stuffed it all—like soiled laundry—in a smelly duffel bag discarded.

It didn't seem to matter that we'd seen the evidence of him dead and gray in that military casket. The belief of a thing is different than the knowing of a thing. The mind believes what it wants, usually in spite of the evidence, not because of it.

The children who grow up thinking God is going to bail on them in the dark of night become adults who don't trust God, people unable to trust God.

I suppose it would be easier not to have believed in God to begin with than to be stuck the way I was—believing that I had been abandoned by him. If you don't believe in the power of something to begin with, then you probably don't miss the absence of it.

But I was a believer from a young age. While other kids carried around bike helmets and skateboards, I carried around a pocket Bible. On rainy days, when the carport became our playground, I'd assume the role of preacher woman.

I've heard it said that everyone has a day of reckoning—a time of crisis when they have to decide whether they will be steadfast believers in things unseen or people who are going to cut and run before the darkness falls. I was only nine when Daddy died. I didn't even know how to spell the word *steadfast*, much less know what it meant.

For far too many years I thought being steadfast in the faith meant a person had to be unwavering in his or her beliefs; that no matter what others were doing or saying, I wasn't going to change my position. I would hold fast to my convictions. That meant that even if God bailed on me, I wasn't going to quit believing in him. I just didn't believe very good things about him. And I certainly didn't believe in his goodness.

It's taken me a lifetime to realize I had it all backwards. God didn't go AWOL when my father died. He wasn't responsible for my father's death at all. The soldier operating the howitzer that morning misfired the gun, causing an explosion in camp and, sadly, killing my father. It wasn't an intentional thing, and for the rest of his life, this veteran felt really bad about my father's death. I don't fault him one bit. For everyone involved I hate that it happened.

But I have come to understand that death is not God's tool. It is not his discipline nor his desire. His love for us is not dependent upon whether we believe in him or whether we believe him to be good.

I still get scared from time to time, about real things and things imagined, but when those moments come, I no longer fear that God is going to cut and run the way I once did. Instead, I recite all the evidence of God's true character, reminding myself, as the psalmist did, that I am not alone.

"He will have no fear of bad news. His heart is steadfast, trusting in the Lord" (Psalm 112:7).

I've come to understand that being steadfast in one's faith does not mean clinging to one's positions, no matter how right or how misguided they may be. It simply means always clinging to the faithful One, no matter what.

Karen Spears Zacharias had her first kiss in a trailer, smoked her first and last cigarette in a trailer, asked Jesus into her heart on bended knee in a trailer, fell madly in love in a trailer (a couple of different times), and gave birth to her first-born child in a trailer. Karen is a former columnist and editorial writer for **The Fayetteville Observer** *in Fayetteville, North Carolina. Her commentary has appeared in* **The New York Times, Newsweek,** *and on* **National Public Radio.** *Her books include* **After the Flag Has Been Folded, Hero Mama, Where's Your Jesus Now,** *and* **Will Jesus Buy Me a Doublewide?** *Learn more about Karen at karenzach.com.*

THE GIRL ON THE COUCH
G.P. TAYLOR

There are just so many ways you can roll a joint. My favorite was always the one that took five pieces of paper rolled together to make a gigantic cone with lots of dope and a little tobacco. I could never understand why people got so uptight about smoking dope. After all, it wasn't heroin, just fun. I didn't see the harm.

Everyone told me it was non-addictive, and it certainly made me feel better. When it came to drugs, I was—and thought I always would be—pro-choice. The more I took, the more I thought everyone should try it. Turn on, tune in, etc. I was sick of politicians saying that they had smoked but never inhaled. Why didn't they just confess and be done with it? After all, it wasn't *that* bad.

Strangely, though, the more I smoked, the more complicated life got.

There was that one time when I missed work. I was employed in the music business, it was the 1970s, and everyone was expected to take days off when the partying had gone too far. But I started to notice that my partying never knew when to stop. It was then that I realized I had an addictive personality. Not that I was an addict to anything in particular, and for sure, I was no junkie.

I was, however, driven to be better, live life faster, and burn brighter than anyone else. The party was an extension of that. I was a workaholic at nineteen, working long hours in a great job and hanging around with people I had seen on television. Work hard then play hard—that was all that mattered to me.

Then came the day that got me thinking about changing things in my life. It was like any other ordinary London day, and it began with a girl. She had stayed the night but remained sober. She had slept on the couch and was different from all the other girls I had known.

"Do you have to do that?" she asked, questioning my desire to live like James Dean. "You can have fun without being stoned."

You would expect a question like that from a preacher, not a girl with black curls, dark jeans, and a baggy shirt. She didn't make a big deal of it but just casually whispered the words between sips of coffee. They hurt. Stopped me dead and started the process that would change my life. Suddenly, I saw an option—I didn't have to behave out of habit. I could be different.

Since I am a man, I wasn't going to give in easily. Hubris should have been my middle name. Image was all-important, and what I did was part of my personality. It was a comfortable little voice, a ring of confidence, a party starter. Giving it up took time. But, circumstances often have a way of intervening in the habits of life and breaking them.

I had a friend, a close friend. She did what I did and had everything under control. Then she met a guy who was a hard-working corporate guy, and together they relaxed. She relaxed so much that within a few weeks she was addicted to heroin. She changed completely. It was frightening to watch as the flesh seemed to drop from her body and she shrunk in size and life.

For the first time in my life I judged someone for what they were doing—not in condemnation but out of concern. I just couldn't let it happen to her, and I certainly wasn't going to go the same way. I couldn't believe I was thinking this way. Totally out of character for me. Instead of just going along with everything, I began to make value judgments about what was good and bad. Before then I didn't really care. Anything goes as long as it doesn't harm anyone else—that was the code I lived by. Now it was all falling apart as I saw how my friend's lifestyle created such devastating consequences for her and everyone around her.

In the circles I traveled in, there were always casualties—Sid and Nancy were the most obvious, living up to the ideal of live fast, die young, and have a good-looking corpse. Those words had been my own mantra along with another that the band Mott the Hoople taught me: "Speed jive, don't want to stay alive when you're twenty-five...."

Change was something I hated, but I realized I had to get out of that place, that town, that life. I could see vast jaws closing in around me, and the only way of escape was on a bus heading north out of London. I was tired of being a slave to what everyone else was doing, but I knew that everyone who was close to me would cast me off as a lunatic if I stopped doing what they did. I would no longer be a part of the tribe, no longer be trusted. But I didn't care; at least I would be alive.

It is amazing how we resist change when we think how others will see us. It can be like a chain holding us tight to actions and habits that we should have stopped long ago.

For me, change of mind meant a complete change of life. I could no longer be with all those friends I once held so dear. Change was big; angry; rough hands coming down and shaking me to the core of my soul. Nothing was left—all was stripped away. It was like dying and losing everything and then waking up in a strange land called *Hometown*, where everything started over again as if I had never left. The strange thing was that I had never been happier.

So who was the girl? I can't even remember her name, and yet in one sentence she changed my life.

G. P. Taylor is a New York Times best selling author. His works include **Shadowmancer, Wormwood, Tersias, The Curse of Salamander Street,** *and* **The Tizzle Sisters.** *He lives on the banks of a river in the midst of a dark wood, an arrow's flight from the Prince Regent Hotel near the 'town at the end of the line'. He spends his days writing and collecting firewood. Learn more about him at gptaylor.info.*

It must have been around 1988. I remember the car my dad drove, and I remember the house we lived in at the time. This is etched in my memory because I specifically remember my dad sitting in his car giving me the *be quiet for a minute, I'm trying to hear something on talk radio* gesture. We have all seen it—the fake strain that communicates we can't quiet hear what is being said with the *pause it* finger in the air. After the gesture and my reluctant cooperation, my Dad proceeded to get out of the car and explain his new position as a *Dittohead*. Dittoheads are loyal Rush Limbaugh listeners who most often respond to Rush's thoughts and ideas with a proud, "I ditto that thought."

My dad was one of Rush Limbaugh's original Dittoheads.

A bright, articulate Dittohead who has influenced me tremendously, Dad started bringing me into the conservative-Republican fold early in life, thanks to his new hero on the airwaves. It all made sense to me, and I saw my parents, my family, and my community flourish in their beliefs and practices. It also didn't hurt that Dad was earning a great living during the Reagan years—it's always easy to embrace an ideology when life is good.

At the same time, my little 5'1", 115-pound (when soaking wet) mother was leading my sister and me in daily devotions directed by Dr. James Dobson. Mom subscribed to every radio series Dr. Dobson ever recorded, which means I've heard them all. I was getting a daily dose of two of the most influential conservative leaders of our time.

Those teachings have served me well, and I continue to embrace many of them today. When you think of conservatism, you typically think of protecting the unborn—I have never been more pro-life than I am now as a father of two children who share my DNA and one Guatemalan princess we adopted. Conservatives have historically stood for small government, low taxes, marriage between one man and one woman, strong military, spanking your kids, capital punishment—you know them all. I said "ditto" to them all...for a while.

In my mid-twenties, I was mentored by a man who told me his story and at the same time made me question everything I believed. Dan Francis was the founding pastor of Crossroads Community Church in Brentwood, Tennessee. I was the second staff person hired, and I accepted the unofficial title of *pastor of etcetera*.

As Dan and I were getting to know each other, we sat at The Puffy Muffin restaurant in Brentwood listening to each other's stories. Sitting across the booth from Dan, I started to sag under the weight of his story. He had a crazy childhood and grew up on the rough side of the tracks. But God transformed his life during his college years. Dan has one of those great stories of rebellion turned to sold-out followership of Jesus Christ.

After God changed his life, Dan was spending some time at his mom's house in Kentucky. One evening a neighbor, high on drugs, started to cause trouble in the front yard. As the older brother and man of the house, Dan went outside to diffuse the issue. As Dan worked to smooth things out, the guy pulled a gun and shot Dan through his chest, puncturing one of his lungs. In an effort to reach Dan and protect him from further harm, Dan's brother ended his own life when he stepped in front of the next bullet.

Dan remembers waking up in the hospital severely injured but suffering even more from the knowledge that his brother was gone—that he had sacrificed his life on Dan's behalf. The way Dan talked about that time in the hospital reminded me of Jacob wrestling with the angel—sheer agony and pain. He told me how he struggled with feelings of anger and hatred on the one hand and living up to his newfound faith by forgiving his brother's killer on the other.

So what were the first thoughts of a son-of-a-Dittohead? I asked, "Did you attend this guy's execution?"

His answer challenged one of the most basic tenets of my conservatism: "No," he calmly responded. "I had no choice but to forgive him, and I actually came to the point where I didn't want him to receive the death penalty."

Oh, come on, Dan. After all, you could save the state some money with just a couple of minutes alone with this creep in his jail cell.

Dan's story began reshaping my thought processes specifically concerning the death penalty and generally everything else I thought I knew about life as well.

Dan gave me enough information that became knowledge (and perhaps wisdom) to think about life in a different way. I believed more than ever in protecting the life of the unborn, but I hadn't thought much about the value of *every* life. All life is created by God. He is the designer and enabler who brings life into existence. Who, then, has the right to extinguish a life other than the Creator of life? Why would a person presume to have that authority? Why would a person even want to get close to such an awesome responsibility?

As a believer in Christ, my first reaction is to turn to Scripture to dig out what it tells us and then align myself to its teachings. But when I turned to the Bible and put those eye for an eye scriptures into context and weighed them against scriptures that teach us to love others as Jesus did, I couldn't find a clear calling for capital punishment.

So, how does a Dittohead change his mind? Not through a political party or a campaign from some special interest group. The catalyst was a trusted friend who shared a view that was different from mine. From there I went through a time of personal reflection where I had to take an honest look at what I believed. The final part of the process was comparing my understanding to Scripture. I came to believe that if I was going to have intellectual integrity, I couldn't choose which lives are valuable and which lives I think I should have power over (even if only through a vote). I have to fight to protect all lives—those of the innocent babies and those of sinful men. In God's economy, the man who killed Dan's brother is no worse a sinner than I.

I am still a card-carrying Republican and even listen to Rush every once in a while, but I depart from the ticket on this issue and others. Dan's story and his convictions challenged my beliefs on the death penalty. More importantly, this change made me realize it's okay to question the things I have been taught by others, especially if those views cannot be supported by Scripture.

These days I'm not so quick to say to my car stereo, "Ditto, El Rushbo." But rather I more often say, "Hmmm. I'll have to think about that."

After several years in the publishing industry, Derek Bell formed Mosaic Trust, LLC, a management consulting firm that specializes in strategic project management, alliance-building, and idea generation. He has worked closely with world-class authors and communicators such as Max Lucado, Brennan Manning, Ravi Zacharias, Stephen Arterburn, and Henry Cloud.

THE DRUM MAJOR SPEECH
PATRICIA RAYBON

I grew up in Colorado in the fifties—black, female, and a little bit odd; out of place in a mostly white world; out of sync with the wild, wild West; out of step with the all-male dominance of the era's power, prestige, and might.

So my beloved parents gave me my marching orders. *Work hard. Be better. Be more.* Claw my way over every stereotype, glass ceiling, high wall, rough obstacle, closed door, and tall fence I was sure to encounter. Quite a few such obstacles blocked my way, indeed.

To fight back, the family game plan—and the message I heard often at our neighborhood Negro church—called for raising my status by focusing on personal ambition. I followed the game plan for years, never quite reaching the elusive goal of great success as measured by the world, but still—by aiming so high—I managed to do quite well.

Now as I sit squarely in middle age, I know my ambition-oriented focus was well intentioned. But it was wrong. Instead, after these many years of life, a little story in the gospels has convinced me the better focus is embodied in one word.

Service.

That should've been the byword for my life. Not this: that by gaining more I'd get more. That by striving to earn, achieve, accomplish, tally up more, I'd gain and prosper even greater. Instead, I now realize that the only way truly to gain and prosper is simply to give.

The paradox is showcased, of course, in the iconic story of Jesus washing his disciples' grimy, dusty feet. Rising up from the wash bowl, Jesus instructed his disciples: "Now that I, your Lord and Teacher, have washed your feet, you also should wash one another's feet" (John 13:14). Or as he added:

"I tell you the truth, no servant is greater than his master, nor is a messenger greater than the one who sent him. Now that you know these things, you will be blessed if you do them" (John 13:16-17).

Can the service mandate get any clearer than that?

Still, I missed the lesson. Even after Dr. Martin Luther King Jr. came on the scene and into prominence—living and teaching the same message that Jesus taught—I still put ambition over altruism; personal gain over selfless giving.

To be honest, I was drawn to Dr. King for his role in tearing down the bigoted power structure seeming to block my path. But, inspired by Jesus, the civil rights warrior prioritized the Gospel message: "Everybody can be great because anybody can serve."

He drove home that point in his "Drum Major" speech, delivered at Ebenezer Baptist Church in Atlanta on February 4, 1968: "If you want to be important—wonderful. If you want to be recognized—wonderful. If you want to be great—wonderful. But recognize that he who is greatest among you shall be your servant. That's a new definition of greatness."

In recent years, I've tried to trade my drum-major instinct— the desire to be seen out front, ahead of others—for the servant definition. But I confess that I struggle. For example, I do a fair amount of *pro bono* work, seeing it as separate. But in truth, all of our work—whether it's selling widgets for profit or writing articles for insight or feeding the poor to fight hunger—should be pro bono, which means *for the good*. (In fact, the full phrase is *pro bono public*: for the public good.)

The bottom line?

Service trumps self. Ambition falls to service. Not this, but that.

I saw that clearly this morning when I opened my e-mail to a slick promo message from Amazon.com, the online book retailer, praising a new lineup of *success in business* books. I scanned the titles and topics and began to understand why so many people make the same mistake I did when I was younger. The e-mail featured books on thinking big, reaching for the sky, climbing past competition—or perhaps the most blatant of the lot, a book about "covert persuasion."

Once, I would've found such titles appealing. I would've paid good money to buy them. I confess that. Now I know this: by loving, by giving, by offering my hands and heart in the shining way of service, I don't find what I seek. I find what Jesus longs to give me.

His all.

Patricia Raybon is author of **My First White Friend,** winner of the Christopher Award "for artistic excellence affirming the highest values of the human spirit," and **I Told the Mountain to Move: Learning to Pray So Things Change,** a 2006 book of the year finalist in **Christianity Today's** book awards' Spirituality category.

IS FAITH AND FILM AN OXYMORON?
RICH PELUSO

I've changed my mind on professional issues many times in my career. I learned early on to think about why I might be wrong before I engage in position battles or in championing an idea or initiative. And in my new career in faith-based film, the mind-changing is happening often. And on one key issue—the role of Christian faith in the arts—the count is three different opinions so far.

Initially I formed the opinion, after fifteen years in Christian music, that film is an even greater delivery device than music for a story with a message. And with a clearly understood and overt path toward God, a film can change hearts and minds. In a world filled with ambiguity, I'd had enough of the opaque and always wanted to hit viewers right on the nose with the Gospel.

Then, after reading several blogs and articles, I started migrating to the idea that faith in film is best delivered through complex stories, situations, and relationships—a well-crafted experience that cleverly delivers truth folded into real-life issues and conflict.

I've spent time listening and talking to those on each side of the spectrum—the hip and earthy Christians who despise and disparage overtly Christian films and the thinly disguised legalistic folks who despise the waste of an opportunity to spell out the spiritual laws and include a virtual altar call in every film. Where do I stand now? I think there is room for both and many shades and layers in between. I've read e-mails from non-believers who were brought to their knees by the simple truth spelled out in an overtly Christian movie, despite the film's creative shortcomings (that the new converts often acknowledge in great detail in their messages). I've also seen the power of subtle storytelling in films like *Bella* and *Les Miserables* bring hardened men to tears.

Film, music, and art in general, like the many other parts of life that fill our days, speak to us in different ways on different days and can sometimes unexpectedly alter our hearts, minds, and life directions. Why do people often try to box God into a set of rules and tools that he is expected to operate within? He can use anything he wants, any time he wants to, to reveal himself and his truth. The key is to focus on a relationship with him that allows space and margin for him to fill with inspiration, direction, and conviction. Through this, we hear our calling to create art that glorifies and reveals him or to experience the creativity of others that does the same. Sometimes a film, song, or book is a clear and bright road sign, lit up with high beams, that says, *God Is Here.* Sometimes they deliver a message with the subtlety of a sunrise, a breath of fresh air, or the parables of Jesus, the greatest artist of all.

Instead of taking sides, I now celebrate any effort to communicate the Gospel through the arts.

After more than fifteen years as a leader within the Christian music industry, Rich Peluso made a midlife career change into the film industry, acquiring and developing faith and family films for Sony Pictures. He lives in the quaint horse-farm community of Leiper's Fork outside of Nashville with his wife and four girls. And a male cat.

STORIES TO KEEP US SANE
MELISSA JENKS

I used to believe that the Bible was true. Completely true—every single word. (In the words of theologians, *inerrant*.)

I now believe that the Bible is true. Completely true—every single word.

So what's changed? I no longer believe that in order to be *absolute* truth, the Bible has to be *literally* true. It doesn't have to mean that earth and life in it were created in seven days. It doesn't have to mean that Methuselah lived for 969 years. It doesn't have to mean that Joshua stopped the sun in the sky or that the streets of heaven are paved with actual gold.

Growing up as a missionary kid in Thailand, I had always wondered why people who believed Scripture was completely literal didn't take Jesus as seriously when he said things like, you know, "Go and sell all your possessions and give to the poor," or, "Do not be anxious for your life, as to what you shall eat, or what you shall drink; nor for your body, as to what you shall put on."

When I came back to the States, to a Christian college, many things were shocking—the snow; the ignorance of my classmates about the rest of the world; the vast quantities of money everyone seemed to have dripping off themselves; the immense amounts they spent on clothes, cars, everything. I thought that those Christians who signed a statement affirming the literal truth of the Bible apparently didn't really believe parts of the Sermon on the Mount.

Reading Scripture made me feel even more stuck. Paul said, "...It was not Adam who was deceived, but the woman being quite deceived, fell into transgression. But women shall be preserved through the bearing of children." I couldn't reconcile that passage with Paul also saying: "There is neither Jew nor Greek, slave nor free, male nor female." I had always believed that I could do anything Christ called me to, but I couldn't reconcile those two verses.

Many of my classmates believed subconsciously that the real job for a Christian woman was to get married and have babies. My female classmates spoke, only half joking, about getting a "ring by spring." Visible terror appeared on their faces at the thought of graduating without good Christian husbands.

As I realized how literalists interpreted what the Bible said about women, I began to feel like my humanity had been taken away from me. At the churches I attended, women were absent from the stage. They were allowed, sure, but Sunday after Sunday, it was men demonstrating for me the image of God. Administrators banned the on-campus Council for Biblical Equality, an organization that tried to advocate scriptural feminism.

I had to make my faith my own, not just thoughtlessly accept everything everyone else said to me, and that deepest part of myself knew I wasn't created as a lesser being. I knew that God designed me as equal. I couldn't reconcile God's true acceptance of me with the belief that what Paul said was completely literal. I had to decide between my full humanity and a specific interpretation of Scripture. If my salvation came only through childbirth, how could God really love me? If I wasn't fully equal, how could I be fully saved?

I didn't find any hope in Bible classes. Instead, I saw Christians throughout history squeezing the words of the Bible to fit their own purposes. The ones who claimed, for instance, that passages on slavery were proof of God's approval of that dehumanizing practice.

Eventually, I settled into agnosticism and nihilism, which brought deep depression and a feeling of emptiness. If I couldn't believe all of it, I decided, I couldn't believe any of it.

Hope appeared during a class with a professor who was also a poet. I discovered that poets have a unique understanding of truth. My professor said she believed the college's statement about Scripture's inerrancy and could sign it in good conscience but that how she interpreted what it said was, maybe, different from someone else's understanding.

She quoted Emily Dickinson: "Tell the truth, but tell it slant."

Jesus, after all, told stories. He was even, maybe, a poet. It took theologians to make a mess of things, to force all the pieces together, to kick out books of the Bible and include others, to write creeds, to excommunicate each other, to justify certain wars and condemn others.

My poet-professor said that every night, each human being goes to sleep and dreams. If we're prevented from sleeping—worse, prevented from dreaming—we go crazy. Unutterably mad. Each of us must tell a story, every night, in order to stay sane. What if the Bible is that kind of story? A story God tells us so we can stay sane? So we can truly live?

It took me years to accept again the core of the Bible's message: Christ came to tell us he loved us, and my only job was to accept that love. Over time, I began to believe that I could accept the love of Abba Father without negating my belief in evolution. I could accept that Jesus died for my sins without figuring out all the details of eternity. I could make it my life's work simply to love God and love others. I could accept the Bible as story—an absolutely true story but a story nonetheless.

At first, I was afraid to tell anyone. When I was finally confident that I could claim a changed Christianity, I began to voice my questions. *What if I can be a Christian without believing everything that you believe?*

It wasn't easy. I had people tell me—even close friends and family—that if I didn't believe the Bible was completely literal, I couldn't be a Christian. I rested on the assurance that all I had to do was, "Believe on the Lord Jesus Christ, and you shall be saved." It's just that simple.

I believe now that it's easier to come to God as a little child. It's easier to accept love without having a list of boxes to be checked off. I've realized that there are many, many Christians who believe as I do, that Christianity is not the closed-off little world that I grew up in.

The poet John Keats may have said it best: "Truth is beauty, beauty truth. That is all you know on earth, and all you need to know."

Melissa Jenks is a writer and professional adventurer who has conquered the Appalachian Trail, large portions of the Pacific Crest Trail, and has tried her hand at open ocean sailing and transcontinental bicycling. She is currently working to save up for her next adventure, which could be anything from building her own log cabin in the wilderness to motorcycling to the southern tip of South America. You can follow her at her blog, casting-off.blogspot.com.

WHY I ABANDONED CHOICE
FREDERICA MATHEWES-GREEN

I was the first feminist in my dorm. It was 1970, and there wasn't a lot of feminism in South Carolina, not even at the state university. I was proud to be one of the pioneers.

One of our goals was to repeal the laws against abortion. I had a bumper sticker on my car: *Don't labor under a misconception: Legalize abortion.* A couple of my friends who had unplanned pregnancies went to New York for abortions, at the time the closest place where it was legal. I cheered them on. Abortion was, to me, proof of feminist commitment, evidence that you would lay your body on the line for the cause of liberation.

Fast forward to January 1976. I was home from grad school for winter break and picked up my Dad's copy of *Esquire*. I came across an essay with an arresting title: "What I Saw at the Abortion." It was written by Richard Selzer, a surgeon and author. In the brief two-page essay, he described how he'd asked a colleague if he could come along the next time he performed an abortion. As a so-called proper-thinking progressive, Selzer supported abortion rights, but he'd never seen a procedure and wanted a better grasp of how it was done.

It was not a typical termination of pregnancy. Most abortions take place in the first twelve weeks, but this patient was nineteen weeks pregnant, in the midst of her second trimester. Selzer described the woman lying on her back on the table, the gentle bulge of her pregnancy evident. The doctor injected her uterus with a hormone to cause labor contractions and left the syringe standing upright there.

Then, Selzer wrote, "I see something other than what I expected here.... It is the hub of the needle that is in the woman's belly that has jerked. First to one side. Then to the other side. Once more it wobbles, is tugged, like a fishing line nibbled by a sunfish."

He realized that what he was seeing was the fetus's struggle for life. Whatever it may have lacked, it did have one thing any human can recognize: a will to live.

As Selzer continued to watch, the agitation of the syringe slowed and then stopped. It seemed he was the only person in the room aware that a death had taken place.

Selzer concluded, "Whatever else is said in abortion's defense, the vision of that other defense will not vanish from my eyes. And it has happened that you cannot reason with me now. For what can language do against the truth of what I saw?"

The "truth of what he saw" disturbed me deeply. I felt strongly about non-violence and opposed war and capital punishment (as I still do today). Had I made an act of violence part of the very foundation of my feminism? If so, it was in ignorance; I really had believed the line that a fetus is "just a glob of tissue." But this was incontrovertible evidence that the fetus had a life independent of its mother.

Though shocked, I could not imagine becoming openly pro-life. Everyone who was cool was pro-choice. I knew pro-lifers only as oddballs—possibly dangerous oddballs—on the evening news.

With time I found the courage to admit my opposition to abortion. I believe that it cost me professionally, that I have lost some opportunities to write because of my pro-life paper trail. But I did what I could and have now spoken on hundreds of college campuses about the feminist, secular argument against abortion. I have written a book on alternatives to abortion and hundreds of articles on the injustice of abortion. I don't think I've had any measurable impact. It's still not cool to be pro-life. There's a limited number of people who will take a stand on an unpopular cause just because they believe it's right. But it's hard for me to think of any injustice more outrageous than violence against the most helpless human beings.

Meanwhile, the abortion number keeps growing; in 2008 it passed the fifty-million mark. Even in my most ardent pro-choice days, I never dreamed the numbers would grow so high. I believe that future generations will judge us on this. It will eventually be impossible to deny that abortion is violence against the helpless. The time to get on the right side of history is now.

By the way, they don't use that injection abortion method that Dr. Selzer saw anymore. The problem was that too often, fetuses were born alive. Most were immediately suffocated or drowned, but it still caused a lot of problems. So that method was replaced with *dilation and evacuation*—the doctor reaches into the uterus with forceps and pulls the unborn apart, like pulling a drumstick off a turkey. But sometimes the ragged ends of the limbs scratched the inside of the uterus, so *intact dilation and evacuation* was developed, in which the fetus was delivered alive, feet first; then the skull was punctured and drained. That method, also called *partial-birth abortion*, caused a lot of controversy, so it's back to the dismemberment method.

How cool is that?

Frederica Mathewes-Green is the author of nine books, most recently **The Jesus Prayer: The Ancient Desert Prayer that Tunes the Heart to God.** *She is a contributor to Beliefnet,* **First Things, Christianity Today,** *and many other publications and speaks at churches, colleges, and conferences across the country. Frederica has been interviewed on* **PrimeTime Live, the Diane Rehm Show, the 700 Club,** *PBS, CNN, NBC, Fox News, and by* **Time, Newsweek, The New Republic, USA Today, Chicago Tribune, Philadelphia Inquirer,** *and* **The New York Times.** *She is the khouria (mother) of Holy Cross Orthodox Church in Linthicum, Maryland, where her husband is pastor. Her Web site is frederica.com.*

CAN YOU ADMIT YOU'RE WRONG?
BOB BUFORD

A decision is a judgment. It is a choice between alternatives. It is rarely a choice between right and wrong. It is at best a choice between 'almost right' and 'probably wrong.'
-Peter Drucker

All of us make decisions—particularly the important ones—with incomplete information. And often, when there's no time pressure, we create urgency by our procrastination. We wait for a special insight or more facts until the last possible moment. We hope that we can somehow predict the future. We look for certainty in the land of probabilities.

The truth is, we can't know until we commit. This is not a new issue. Aristotle, the most pragmatic of all the philosophers, spoke of this decision sequence: know → understand → desire → choose.

Simple, but brilliant. Too often people seem to find themselves frozen on the trigger, unable to choose and commit. It's not a new disease.

So, when faced with a go or no go deadline, you do choose—
you do pull the trigger—you do commit yourself. Then you get
more knowledge, lots more knowledge.

In the early 1980s, I made what could have been a "bet your
company" decision to enter the subscription television business
(essentially a one-channel-over-the-air pay TV business) in three
big cities: Cincinnati, Chicago, and Minneapolis. In those days
my company, Buford Television, operated network television
stations in small markets like Tyler, Texas, and Fort Smith, Ar-
kansas. My big-time Washington law firm, which represented
a network and some other major players, advised me to go for
subscription TV. After toiling away for twenty years (quite pro-
ductively, I might add) in small markets, this was a chance to
make a quantum leap into the big leagues. By supplying a movie
channel over the air, I could get the jump on cable TV in big cities
and make a lot of money in a hurry. In my early forties, I was hot
to do just that—to be an instant Ted Turner!

We acquired television licenses in these three cities and
scoured the country for more. We put new stations on the air
in Cincinnati and Chicago—me and my guys from little Tyler and
Fort Smith! Almost from day one, I was haunted by two over-
powering emotions: excitement and fear. Excitement in the
sense of *this is a great chance to get rich quick.* And a deeply felt
but certainly un-confessed fear that we small-town boys didn't
know what we were doing. We promptly went from zero to
eight hundred employees. And of course, we didn't really know
any of these new hires, even the managers. We were spending a
fortune on advertising, a call center, and an antenna installation
force. Soon enough, we discovered that big northern metropoli-

tan, multi-ethnic areas weren't like our comparatively small towns. I felt like Dorothy in *The Wizard of Oz* ("This isn't Kansas, Toto!"). The business took off with early adopters, but we had no idea how permanent these new subscribers were. Sleepless nights ensued. Deep in the pit of my stomach, I knew we were in over our heads.

Uh oh! What do you do when the facts of a decision tell you that you took the wrong road? Two pieces of wisdom were pivotal—one from Jack Welch, the other from the writings of Oxford don C.S. Lewis.

Lewis said (paraphrased), "When you come to a fork in the road and find you have taken the wrong road, don't keep pressing forward trying to prove you were right (a particularly male disease). You promptly (and painfully) turn back to the fork in the road and embark on the right road."

And I had read that Jack Welch completely changed the direction of GE (certainly one of the most successful companies of his generation) based on a single question from Peter Drucker: "If you weren't in that line of business today, would you get into it now? If the answer is 'no,' then the decision is clear: Get out."

That's just what I did. It was a painful blow to my overheated ego, and it cost my company a million dollars. But it ultimately cost the company I sold these stations to $72 million. The subscription TV business skyrocketed at first then went bust all over the country. Meanwhile, I was free to go on to other, more profitable ventures.

Most of the things that determine the success of an undertaking—whether a business, government, or nonprofit—are beyond our control. Markets rise and decline unpredictably. We constantly misperceive how others will react to what we do.

So what do you do when you have gotten, with the best of intentions, into a business relationship—or perhaps a personal friendship—that turns out to be a bad deal, a quagmire, a fiasco? You pray that the tide will turn; you give it second chances, third chances, and even fourth chances. You tough it out for a while, sometimes a long while. It's often more difficult to get out than to get in.

But you don't persist forever in a state of denial. You confront what my wise author friend Jim Collins calls "the brutal facts." You don't decide based on just feelings. If the facts prove that you're still on the wrong track, you bite the bullet, pay the price, and find something better to do. You get out.

When the horse is dead, dismount.

Bob Buford is the founder of Halftime, an organization devoted to helping people make the transition from success to significance, and Leadership Network, which provides resources and counsel to pastors of large churches. He is the author of several books, including **Half Time** *(Zondervan).*

A few years back, my husband was a well-respected physician at the top of his career—director of emergency services and chief of medical staff. He loved taking care of patients, and I loved caring for our family. We lived in a picture-perfect town in a three-story New England house, enjoying the good life and living the American dream.

But something was missing. We had all the nice things that were supposed to make us happy, yet at the core we still felt hollow.

Around this time, we went on a family vacation to a barrier island off the coast of Florida. The island is idyllic—no cars, no roads, no stores—just sun and surf and beautiful sunsets. When the kids went to bed, I asked two questions that would change our lives forever.

"What do you think is the biggest problem facing the world today?"

After a few minutes, Matthew offered a reply that I was not expecting: "The world is dying. If we don't have a healthy planet to sustain humanity, none of the other problems will matter."

The more we talked about the demise of the planet, the more depressing it all felt. The problems seemed so overwhelming. That's when I asked the second, more difficult, question: "If the planet is dying, what are we going to do about it?"

My husband did not have a ready answer. A couple of months later, he finally did get back to me—with an answer I wasn't prepared to hear:

"I'll quit my job," he said, "and put all my energy toward saving the planet."

"Are you sure we need to do that much?" I replied.

I had always thought of myself as a good environmentalist. But giving up a career that my husband clearly loved, as well as the prestige, steady income, and security that came along with it, to "save the planet"?

The thought terrified me. My stomach turned inside out just thinking about what we might lose—our beautiful home, our harborside neighborhood, our vacations—not to mention health benefits and a retirement plan.

The selfish part of me began to whine: what about the three years of undergraduate school, four years of medical school, and three years of residency we had gone through together? Wouldn't he be wasting all that training (and money)? And then there were practical concerns: how would we possibly save enough money to pay for our children's education if our income dropped suddenly to zero? How, for that matter, would we put food on the table?

Each of my arguments sounded logical on its own. In the material world, my husband's sudden career change made no sense. Walking in faith may sound good in theory—when it happens to other people and everything turns out okay in the end—but I was terrified to take even the first step. What followed was a tense time, full of anxiety, fear of change, and conflicting desires.

People ask us if we had any arguments. Of course we did! I'd be lying if I said that there were no raised voices or sleepless nights. But gradually I came, if not to peace, at least to acceptance of the new direction our lives would take.

Providentially, as we embarked on our environmental journey, we also began a faith journey. It seemed—at least to us—that the two were inseparable. One slow night in the hospital, Matthew picked up a Gideon's Bible in the waiting room and started to read it. He brought it home and we both began reading it. One by one, each of us became believers—and that changed everything. Suddenly, our whole family was working off the same page. We had a clear purpose: to love God with all our hearts, minds, souls, and strength, and to love our neighbors as ourselves. One way that we could show our love for the Creator and for our global neighbors was to start taking better care of the planet.

We took Jesus' advice in Matthew 7 and began cleaning up our own acts before worrying about cleaning up the rest of the world. Over the next couple of years, we reduced our electricity usage and trash production by nine-tenths and our fossil fuel usage by two-thirds. After we had our own house in order, we felt called to share our journey.

Today, when making any choice, purchase, or decision, we ask ourselves two new questions: *Does this bring me closer to God?* And, *Does this help me love my neighbor?*

The answers always lead us down the right path.

Nancy Sleeth is Program Director of Blessed Earth (blessedearth.org) and author of **Go Green, Save Green: A Simple Guide to Saving Time, Money, and God's Green Earth** *(Tyndale 2009). Her husband, Matthew Sleeth, MD, is author of* **Serve God, Save the Planet** *(Zondervan 2007) and* **The Gospel According to the Earth: Why the Good Book Is a Green Book** *(HarperOne 2010) as well as creator of* **Elements,** *a twelve-film creation care series (Zondervan 2010).*

PLAYING THE FOOL'S GAME
CAMERON CONANT

At twenty-two years of age, as a newly minted college graduate, I had it all figured out: whom I was going to marry, what my politics were, and why I was a Christian. Of course, looking back on it now, these things seem more like bluster than beliefs. Beneath my over-confident façade was a frightened kid who just wanted to be taken seriously. Sure, I knew the adage about college kids naively thinking they know it all. But at the conservative college I attended, "knowing it all" meant that you stood for something.

I wanted to stand for something, so I put my stake in the ground and got married, got baptized, and got outspoken about my Republicanism. At the time, these things were the unofficial holy trinity of American evangelicalism—or at least of the evangelical tradition with which I was familiar—and they solidified my credentials as an appropriate person to combat the secular assault on faith, family, and free markets. I wanted to be a soldier in God's army, and I became that by arguing my beliefs with an almost militarized gusto.

As a newspaper reporter, I constantly questioned my editor's decisions: *Why did you place that article* (which amounted to an overly critical editorial on our Republican president) *on the front page of the paper?* I sometimes launched scathing verbal attacks on those with whom I disagreed politically and sarcastically referred to CNN as "Clinton News Network." I regularly listened to conservative talk radio and became angry about things I hadn't even thought to be angry about before. I became almost obsessed with having a fully integrated "Christian worldview" in order to separate right belief from wrong belief, the sheep from the wolves, the conservatives from the liberals. I was on the front lines of the conservative culture wars—or so I thought—until something unexpected happened.

My wife left and filed for divorce.

There was no discussion about her leaving, just a note on the table with a few keys placed next to it. She took half the furniture, half the silverware, half of everything. My confident façade had been laid bare, and things that once seemed so important no longer mattered. There was no energy left to argue politics or evaluate the minutiae of everyday life through the lens of a Christian worldview. I began to realize that I was the emperor, and the emperor had no clothes. My empty political creeds and surface-level religious notions were strangely anachronistic. The world had changed. Years passed in a moment.

Yet unbeknownst to me then, I was finally on the path to true spiritual transformation. A writer I like says that the only paths to true spiritual transformation are prayer and suffering. And it's true: in the crucible of suffering, we stop enslaving ourselves to the ego, which must always be right, and are instead given a great gift—the opportunity to find our true selves, centered in God.

All these years later, I realize that a life centered in God—what I would call true Christian spirituality—looks nothing like dogmatism. It doesn't look like sarcasm either, nor does it look like an ascent, with its triumphal messages of wealth, dominance, and prosperity.

Instead, I think it looks more like a lowly fool's game in which the last are first; where it's difficult for the wealthy, arrogant, and powerful to see clearly; where God's politics are neither liberal nor conservative but instead concerned with the least of these; where radical love, acceptance, and forgiveness are the norm; where, without love, we are as noisy as an errant car alarm—or a boorish twenty-two-year-old who criticizes those around him before ever taking the time to listen or experience what he's talking about.

I've also learned from my experience and the experiences of others that in the absence of any true spiritual growth, what often takes root in the religiously minded person (Christian or otherwise) is an opposition mentality in which a villain must be identified, attacked, and eliminated. And this makes sense, for if we are not living in love, we will usually live in fear—a characteristic that some have suggested is actually the opposite of love (rather than hate). And if God is love, and perfect love casts out all fear, then it stands to reason that the fearful person, with his or her imagined enemies, will always be discordant and out of tune with God.

I saw a bumper sticker recently that brought this division between fear and love into stark relief. It read, *Religion is for those who don't want to go to hell; spirituality is for those who have already been there.* To which I say, amen and amen.

May we all learn this lesson sooner rather than later. Our lives are too short to waste on being divisive, fearful, and angry. We serve a loving God who invites everyone to his table—liberals, conservatives, illegal immigrants, divorcées, thieves, capitalists, socialists, communists, and people of all ethnicities. Just don't bring your fear or your pride. It's of no use in this backwards kingdom of grace.

Cameron Conant is a former newspaper reporter and magazine editor. He is the author of two books, including **With or Without You** *(Relevant Books) and* **The Year I Got Everything I Wanted** *(NavPress). Currently, Cameron is on a two-year assignment with the Peace Corps in Cape Verde, a chain of islands in the Atlantic Ocean off the north coast of Africa. When he can get to his town's Internet café, he blogs about this and other things at cameronconant.blogspot.com.*

JESUS AFTER SUNDAY SCHOOL
R.N. FROST

I grew up in church, so I knew a few things about Jesus. To me, he was the divine bastion of the status quo. Not someone I was interested in. He personified every moral demand a nervous adult could think up; therefore, he was a God figure I could do without. For many of my younger years, I kept him at a distance. But I've had a heart change since then, and I now find him to be absolutely captivating. Here's what happened.

Dave was a high school classmate of mine who got a motorcycle on his sixteenth birthday and was killed on it a few weeks later. Losing a friend was bad enough, but the response of my classmates made it worse. There were tears and hugs at first, but we had a party the following Friday. Not for his sake—it was what we did every Friday night. One minute we were hearing somber platitudes about Dave; then it was time to party.

It just didn't feel right, so I walked out. Another friend, Tom, was also leaving, so I asked him where he was going.

"I can't handle this," he explained. "Dave just died and we're all a bunch of jerks acting like he never existed."

So we talked—just a couple disillusioned guys asking the big questions: *Why are we here? Who cares if we die?* I'm not sure how we got there, but somehow we came to the conclusion that maybe God makes a difference. We weren't even sure he really existed—it was a gut response that announced the end of my Sunday school version of Jesus. As far as I had been concerned, I was no longer a Christian.

I really hadn't abandoned the idea of God, but I was skeptical about the version of God I grew up with—Jesus included. In the following months of my new post-Christian life, I began quietly looking in new directions.

My father retired from the Air Force that summer, and we left Montana as he looked for a new job. After a month and thousands of miles on the road, some spontaneous, unplanned choices placed us back in Montana in our two-car caravan, heading for Spokane. I was in the car with my folks for a change, instead of back with my older brother in his car. Mom announced the next town, "Here comes Big Timber."

"That's the town that leads to the church camp where you sent me last summer," I said.

"Would you like to go visit?" she asked.

We agreed to go, even though I wasn't campaigning for it. In fact, it felt a bit weird. If I had been back with my brother in our Volkswagen, we would have sailed right through Big Timber. It was just one more oddity in a series of odd circumstances. We hadn't even planned on being back in Montana.

Things got even stranger when we arrived at the camp and discovered that the high school work crew had just lost two male staff members who had suddenly quit. Within the hour my brother and I, as instant replacements, waved goodbye to our family. It felt very weird!

Two weeks later, during the high school camp, I was picked—without my consent—to be a spiritual leader for a couple dozen of the other campers. Not a good role for a post-Christian kid.

What should I do? I took my Bible and went off campus to have a talk with God. I felt like a puppet, and I wanted to talk to the puppeteer.

"God, if you're there I need to hear from you!" Silence.

"If you're there, I know I can't barge in on you. But if you're a good God, and if you're behind my being here, you've gotta answer me." More silence. Birds, clouds, and flowers all around me in a beautiful valley.

An hour went by. Then out of nowhere a thought came: *Hey, dummy, if you want to hear from God, try reading your Bible!* My inward response was that I already knew what it said! But I started reading anyway, in Matthew.

In the Sermon on the Mount, Jesus was waiting for me. He confronted my sin. I was guilty as charged. He told me I can't serve two masters—I would love one and hate the other. Caught again. I had been playing games with God, blaming him for my own stuff. But how would I serve him? I had to make a living, didn't I? I then read about his care for the birds of the air and the flowers of the field: *Won't he take care of you, you man of little faith?* Ouch.

So what did he want from me?

He answered: *Seek first the kingdom of God and his righteousness—then let him deal with all your concerns.*

I bowed my heart and said, "Okay, I'm yours."

Up until then, Jesus had been the lead character in a bunch of Sunday school stories. I knew *about* him but never really *knew* him. What I thought I knew of him came from well-intentioned people who turned the Gospel into a set of rules. But on that day when I looked for him in the Bible, I actually met *him*—not what others had told me about him.

And that made all the difference.

R.N. Frost was a professor in Bible and spiritual life at a college and seminary in Portland, Oregon, for twenty years. He is now with Barnabas International and travels worldwide to teach and encourage other followers of Christ. Ron posts a weekly blog at spreadinggoodness.org.

NO TRICK-OR-TREATING!
KATHERINE CALLAHAN-HOWELL

When I moved to an urban neighborhood from my suburban background to start a new church, I discovered that satanic worship existed as a dramatic force in my new environment. Blood sacrifices of cats and other rituals happened in the same neighborhood as our new church plant. As I see this in written form, it sounds like fiction. But it's not.

Halloween, that harmless holiday I had so enjoyed as a child had, in our neighborhood, become the high holy day of the enemy of our souls. As a pastor and parent, I felt it could be unsafe for our children to go out trick or treating in this environment, so our church offered an All Saints party as an alternative activity. We wanted to provide a fun, safe, and Christian option to the night of mischief outside our doors.

But I took it a step further. I wrote a letter to our congregation explaining why we did not sanction trick-or-treating or any recognition of this holiday, basically forbidding my congregants to participate in this secular concession and invitation to evil. I fully expected all their children to attend our alternative party.

Now truthfully, the satanic connection to Halloween in our area still exists, and I find it as disgusting and spiritually dangerous as ever. But as the years rolled by, I began to realize I should not dictate how the people of our church should respond to this holiday.

I came to see that the possible harmless fun I enjoyed as a child still existed and should not be legislated against. At some point I asked my older children if they would object to my allowing my youngest to trick-or-treat. I know that when parents change policies midstream, it can create a sense of unfairness or betrayal: "How come *he* gets to do that? You never let *me* do it?" Thankfully my children maturely agreed to the change, graciously allowing me to learn from my mistakes and make a change for the benefit of their brother, who got to participate in an activity they did not.

Quite frankly, I still don't like Halloween because of its pagan origins and the fact that members of satanic cults consider it their highest holy day. But I no longer feel it is right for me to force this view on others. I know that many Christian traditions use the holiday to focus on their departed saints and other loved ones and that others feel it is a harmless tradition. As a church leader, I am more comfortable now with leading by example than dictum. This applies to other issues, much more pervasive than this once-a-year event. For example, although I have strong views against abortion, capital punishment, and the practice of homosexuality, I am less likely to push my agenda on others. Instead, I have become more concerned about how the church treats the young woman with an unwanted pregnancy, the family of an incarcerated individual, or the same-sex couple who move into our neighborhood.

Tolerance is not a Christian virtue, but compassion is. We need to love all people and let the Holy Spirit convict them if they fall into sin. And regardless of how we view another's behavior, we are always called to be messengers of grace.

I don't regret forming an alternative to trick-or-treating for the children in our neighborhood and church. I believe it has protected our children from physical and spiritual harm. Besides, we've had a lot of fun at those All Saints parties. What needed changing were my efforts to dictate how everyone else thought about Halloween. Too many church leaders are unwilling to admit they are wrong. I don't want to be that kind of leader.

Katherine Callahan-Howell serves as founding pastor of the Winton Community Free Methodist Church in Cincinnati, Ohio. She is an ordained elder in the Free Methodist Church with a master's in divinity from Asbury Theological Seminary. Callahan-Howell authored a book entitled **Spiritual Exercises for Couch Potatoes** *as well as articles in publications such as* **Leadership Journal** *and writes a prayer column for* **Light and Life** *magazine. She and her husband, Roger, enjoy four children, Nora, Junia, Luke, and Wesley, who are now all too old to trick-or-treat.*

HOW TO KEEP GOD FROM GETTING BORING
BILL MYERS

180

By the time I was in high school, I was so bored with God I could hardly stand it. As far as I was concerned, the Christian life was about as exciting as bowl of oatmeal. A friend challenged my assessment, saying God was so vanilla to me because I was only partly Christian. I had the salvation stuff all down but knew nothing about Christ as my Lord, or boss.

I said, "So what am I supposed to do?"

He said, "If you promise always to say 'yes' to God, regardless of how stupid it sounds or how you're sure he doesn't know what he's talking about, your life will be anything but boring."

It was probably the best advice I've ever received. I was young and stupid and naïve, so I agreed to do as he suggested, and it changed all my thinking about God being boring.

Fast forward to the University of Washington. For most of my life, I had planned to be a dentist. Imagine me in a theater watching only the fourth movie of my life. (I grew up in the Cascade Mountains and didn't get out much.) I'd seen *Pollyanna*, *The Parent Trap*, and *Pinocchio*. Now I was watching *The Godfather*. I couldn't believe what I was seeing. More sobering was the way my peers were leaping to their feet and cheering when human lives were being slaughtered.

I left that theater feeling absolutely astonished at the power of drama to manipulate people's emotions and told God he better get on the ball and raise people up in this area. But every time I told him what he had to do, it came back at me that I was supposed to be one of those people. It was ridiculous—I didn't even know how to *watch* a movie, let alone *make* one. But after several weeks arguing and because of that promise I made, I finally said, "All right, I'll try to make movies."

Slight problem: No film school in the country would take me. The only school that said yes was in Rome, Italy. Soon I found myself in a country whose language I couldn't speak, studying a subject I knew nothing about. Foolish? You bet. Boring? Not in the slightest.

Later, I moved to Los Angeles to become a rich and famous film director and discovered they had plenty of those and didn't need any more. So I proceeded to starve. Actually, I didn't starve; I just became an expert at eating macaroni and cheese. I was crying out to God, saying, "I'll do anything for you—well, except write because I got Cs and Ds in my one writing class in college and have read a grand total of three books for pleasure. But anything else, you just name it."

At the time I was directing a play in Hollywood (for free). A producer saw it and asked if I would write for his TV series. I asked if it paid, and he said yes, so I said, "Sure, no problem," then raced home and had a good cry and panic attack.

I wrote the TV show, and it was so bad that when I watched it I reached down, picked up a shoe, and threw it at the set. It was awful. Terrible! But it was the only game in town, so I wrote another. This time the studio was smart enough not to buy it. I wrote another and another. No sale.

Not long afterward, a publisher back east who had heard I was a TV writer asked if I would write a book for them. I ask if it paid. He said it did. "Sure, no problem." I had another crying and panic attack and wrote the world's worst book. It was awful. Terrible! And today, when hotshots interview me and ask me the title of my first book, my answer is always the same: "Next question, please."

Anyway, I wrote another book, and, for whatever reason, the publisher bought it. And another, and they bought that one too. And gradually, painfully slowly, my work stopped stinking. That was 104 books ago, before forty national and international awards.

The key to my success is that I'm a coward, I'm a crybaby, and I'm untrained. But I've agreed to say yes to whatever I feel God wants. And because it seems there are so few Christians in the country willing to do that, he has to use whomever he can get.

Sometimes I think it's like we've all entered the stadium. We've got our tickets that say: *Salvation*. We take our seats and Jesus is down on the field saying, "Glad you're here, come on down and play." But all my friends are so worried that he'll disrupt and turn their lives around that they just sit in the stands for ten, twenty, fifty years, bored out of their skulls. Meanwhile, a few of us (often the most unqualified), are naïve enough to stumble out onto the field and play.

I used to think being a Christian was boring. But because I took a chance with some advice from a friend, I discovered that God is full of surprises if you will just listen to him and obey him. My whole life has been a series of chances. I honestly don't know what God's got for me next. Is it scary? It's terrifying. But if you put yourself completely in God's hands, I can promise you two things: he'll never drop you, and it will never be boring.

Bill Myers is a prolific writer and filmmaker whose books and videos have sold more than five million copies. He has won more than forty national and international awards for his work. He created the popular and award-winning series, **The Adventures of McGee and Me,** *and the teen fiction* **Forbidden Door** *series. Learn more about Bill at billmyers.com.*

CAN A LEADER BE NICE?
MARK OESTREICHER

I had convinced myself that I was speaking the truth; whether it is spoken "in love" or not, speaking the truth is what leaders are supposed to do. But the young woman in my office started crying, and something tipped sideways in my self-analysis.

This crying young woman represented the third meeting in a single day, all in my office, where I had spoken "the truth" to someone, only to have them end up in tears. After the first of these meetings, I felt a rush of power—confident that I was doing what leaders do. After the second, my confidence waned a bit, and I had an inner Scooby Doo saying, *Huh?* But that third meeting? It started me on a path of change.

I've always been a leader who was willing to be vocal with my thoughts and opinions (much to the frustration of many others in my life). On those spiritual gifts tests, I always scored a flat-lined zero in the area of mercy. And here's the silly part: I was proud of that.

When I worked in a church that was going through a massive transition, I was asked to be on a transitional leadership team and was taken under the wings of the two older pastors leading the process. They were both naturally gifted leaders but had similarly convinced themselves of the strength of their weaknesses. In fact, I remember to this day the exact wording of the mentoring I received from the two of them in one meeting.

They said, "Marko, your lack of mercy is the strength of your leadership."

Hey, that sounded good to me (embarrassing and stupid as it sounds to me today). And for the next few years, I steamrolled people left and right under the ruse of "strong biblical leadership."

But that crying young woman loosened something in me. And through divine revelation or long overdue common sense (or some combination of both), I immediately knew I needed to change. But I had no idea how to make that happen even though I was accustomed to making everything happen in my world.

I carefully selected two older men whom I perceived to be strong yet merciful leaders and asked them to mentor me in the areas of mercy and gentleness. At one of my first meetings with one of these guys, he stated the should-have-been obvious: I couldn't *make* myself have mercy; I could only ask God to give me mercy and pursue a life of mercy. The other guy helped me understand something that became a framing idea for me: I'll likely never score high in mercy on spiritual gifts tests; but I can still grow in mercy. This same dynamic plays out in all areas of my life: I'll never be perfect, but I'm still called to righteousness; I'll never love perfectly, but I'm still called to be loving.

These two new understandings reframed leadership and mercy for me and put me on a multi-year quest for change. I met with these mentors; I read books on mercy (and the kind of leadership that was more Jesus-y than CEO-like); I journaled and prayed; and I asked friends to help me.

About two years later (yes, it took that long!), I received a great double confirmation from God that I was making progress. One day, I had someone comment to me (someone who didn't know of my quest) how gentle they thought I was. I could hardly believe someone would ever use that word to describe me. Then, a few days later, one of the secretaries of the church told me that the other secretaries had a nickname for me: the gentle steamroller. I laughed out loud when I heard this: yup, I still had that steamroller way about me at times; and I'm not even sure what a "gentle steamroller" would be. But I responded, "Hey, I'll take that!" It was the best compliment I'd received in a long time.

As I write this, it's eleven years later. I'm still a merciless jerk on a regular basis. I am still very capable of possessing the gentleness of a sledgehammer from time to time (and even of being momentarily proud of it!). But I can see change. I wish it were more immediate. The only thing that was immediate was my recognition of the need for change. The process of change has been and will continue to be a long, slow journey of transformation.

Mark Oestreicher has been involved in church ministry, particularly working with teenagers and youth workers, for much of his life. Until recently, Marko served as president of Youth Specialties in San Diego, an organization that trains and equips church youth workers. He has authored or contributed to more than 50 books, including **Youth Ministry 3.0,** *and his most recent work* **Middle School Ministry.** *Marko speaks nationally and internationally, and consults with churches, publishers and other businesses. An active blogger with 2000 daily readers, Marko is engaged in social media and is a forward thinker in all things digital and youth.*

THE FIGHT TO BE RIGHT
BECKY ROBBINS-PENNIMAN

My college major was cognitive psychology—not the touchy-feely stuff but hard science. I was taught the scientific method so I could find the right answer, the truth.

From college I went to law school. I was taught to research, strategize, and argue to win cases. In law, establishing the truth is not only about being right; it's also about proving the other side wrong.

In my Christian faith, the stakes are even higher than in science or law. I was taught that we need to decide who and what is right because God demands it and gave us a book with the right answers in it. If you were wrong, you didn't just lose; you were damned. Certainty equaled salvation.

So for many years, I wanted to be right more than anything. However, as I got more experience in life, I began to be suspicious of that desire. I began to understand that there are big differences between being correct and being right. *Correctness* is about independently verifiable facts—everything from phone numbers to historical dates. Being correct is usually good and useful.

But being *right* is different. Being right is about pitting one set of opinions and perspectives against another and declaring a winner. I began to ask a question that many of those who had taught me wished to avoid: *Is there an inherent reason why our perspective is more valid? Isn't it arrogant to insist that our point of view is right just because it is ours?*

After fifteen years of practicing law, I went to seminary. There we studied epistemology, the branch of philosophy concerned with the nature and origin of knowledge. Epistemology asks the question, *How do we know what we know?* Surprisingly, knowledge—that which is considered to be "right" in a culture or a religion—is usually subjective, and is "that which is consistent with the viewpoint held most widely among those with power in the group." Often that dominant viewpoint solidifies and becomes what is natural, normal, and desirable in that group and is the standard of knowledge against which all other opinions are judged. In religion, the dominant viewpoint can be elevated to be the test of orthodoxy.

Just because rightness is subjective, however, doesn't mean it's wrong or bad to be committed to what we believe is right. In fact, in order to navigate the world, we need to have a personal sense of what is right, a truth that we think is worthy of our trust, of giving our hearts to, and to use as the foundation for deciding how to live.

The question becomes, *What is our attitude toward those whose truth is different from ours?* One approach is the triumphalism of many in my culture and faith tradition, where other points of view and those who believe differently are not only wrong but unnatural, abnormal, undesirable, heretical, and in need of defeat.

However, another approach is courageous humility. In this attitude, we honor the integrity of those who hold to a different truth while affirming the value and authenticity of the truth we know. Humility leaves open the possibility that we don't know everything and just might learn something from those who have a different perspective. When our humility is *courageous*—literally, from the heart—our lives are deeply committed to the truth we hold dear, yet there is no associated need to prove anyone else's truth to be wrong.

One event, when I was a staff attorney with a state agency, made me deal with the tensions among being right, being courageous, and being humble. An employee in the agency had pled guilty to but had in fact not committed a misdemeanor. The agency's director insisted we take action to place a censure in the employee's work record. Given the guilty plea, a case would have been easy to develop and was the "right" thing to do to protect the agency's interests. However, the personal suffering and career damage it would cause to an innocent employee were incalculable.

I was faced with the choice of whether I would do the "right" thing or what was *actually* right and be committed to the values of my faith (i.e., to Christ's commandment to be merciful). Although it made the director angry, I declined to develop the agency's case. However, humility required me to acknowledge that the director and the staff attorney who took the case could have been just as committed to their Christian faith as I was.

As I continue my Christian spiritual journey, I'm finding less and less need to prove that others are "wrong," even those embracing different religions. As I've changed my mind about the need to be right, compassion has become more important, faith has become more hopeful, truth has become more beautiful, and following Christ has become an exciting adventure.

Becky Robbins-Penniman is an Episcopal priest serving the Lamb of God Church in Ft. Myers, Florida.

WHO'S GOING TO HELL?
HAROLD IVAN SMITH

I grew up in a community of faith that took hell seriously. "Go to hell!" was not merely an expletive. In those days before air conditioning, on many hot Sunday nights, Brother AJ and Brother Sam, our pastors, tackled hell. Periodically, the "traveling firemen" (evangelists) would out-hell our pastors! You could smell smoke! Hellfire-and-damnation preachers prided themselves on "telling it like it is!" They, unfortunately, were hell heavy, grace "lite."

Leaving my grandfather's funeral one hot Indiana afternoon, I heard Uncle Carl bellow, "If it's this hot in hell, I sure don't want to go." Some family members thought he was hell destined and had been the preacher's homiletic bullseye. Otherwise, why would Brother Emert preach on hell at a funeral?

Some Christians, apparently, will not be happy in heaven if hell is not running over!

As a young child, I could not get the hell the pastors preached to reconcile with my Sunday school teachers' expositions on Jesus, the Good Shepherd. Sunday after Sunday, they tried to help children wrap their minds around grace.

For years, that threat of eternal damnation kept me from taking communion because of that severe biblical passage, "He or she that eateth or drinketh unworthily...." As a sensitive adolescent, the threat of eternal damnation led me to a *better not partake* decision. That fixation distracted me from the wideness of God's mercy we sang about.

Then one night, in my late twenties, in a small group Bible study, my friend Jerry Hull explained that the only persons who are unworthy are those who think they are worthy!

While writing this article, I pondered the twists and turns in the process of changing my mind on hell.

The change began when my pastor during my teen years, Eudell Milby, skipped opportunities to preach on hell. He instead pointed to grace "deep and wide."

Graduate school was a blowtorch on my frozen, easy-answer theology. My professors, all committed Christians, nudged my certainty on eternal themes. Professor Walter Towner invited his students to embrace William Faber's hymn, "There's a wideness in God's mercy."

"For the love of God is broader

Than the measure of our mind;

And the heart of the Eternal

Is most wonderfully kind"

In a meeting with pastors examining candidates for district licenses, in response to their questions, I shared my beliefs. The man running the meeting abruptly ended our time by praying, "O Lord, we know some of our young people go off to liberal graduate schools and get mixed up about their faith!" (I was not ordained.)

Still, "There's a wideness in God's mercy" became my theological mooring.

Then one day in doctoral studies, lightning struck with a professor's observation that hymnal editors are cautiously selective. Hence, congregations rarely sing—or want to sing—all the verses that had originally flowed from the hymnist's imagination. There are the left-out verses. One day I discovered "the rest of the hymn."

"But we make His love too narrow

By false limits of our own;

And we magnify His strictness

With a zeal He will not own."

Over the years in professional ministry, I have kept my doubts about hell to myself. I have lip-serviced a worn motto, "There's a heaven to gain and a hell to shun." In 2009, when I was invited to speak at the University of Wisconsin's grief conference, I chose hell for my presentation. Because I would be speaking to

practitioners of a wide array of faiths—and nonbelievers—I wres-
tled: *What do I believe? What am I willing to admit I believe?* Too
commonly these days, skeptical listeners seize one thing with which
they disagree and spin it out of proportion. Quite candidly, I did not
want to be branded *soft on hell.* It is permissible to sing, "and grace
will lead me home" as long as you acknowledge it is not going to
lead everyone home!

Pondering hell depleted some of the sureness I had had about
people who did not fit my theological constrictions.

"When we all get to heaven," we are going to be stunned by the
magnitude of God's grace! Heaven will have a transitional pouting
room for those who cannot be as generously wide as God.

It is important to be open to change because God's mercy is
beyond all our notions, ideas, theories, dogmas, doctrines. Faber
nailed it: "There is a wideness in God's mercy!"

Yeah, there is a hell whose guest roster is God's business and
not mine. My task is to sing, live out, and to share the outrageous
wideness in God's mercy.

*Harold Ivan Smith is a grief educator, writer, and popular speaker. He is a member
of the teaching faculty at St. Luke's Hospital in Kansas City, Missouri, where he leads
Grief Gatherings—innovative storytelling groups. He has written many books on
grief, including* **The ABCs of Healthy Grieving** *and* **When a Child You Love Is
Grieving***.*

REEVALUATING THE CORNER OFFICE
JOHN R. GERLACH

I began my career in the publishing industry after graduating from college in 1980. My first job was with a paperback book publisher as a sales representative. A year and a half into my career, a corporate sale of the paperback book division resulted in the termination of the entire sales force. Fortunately, I was offered a position within the magazine division. Apparently I had made a big enough impression with management to secure a position.

Shortly thereafter, a sales position opened with a very prestigious magazine publisher. After extensive interviews, I was offered a position. Although the salary was less than my current position, I felt the future growth potential was greater with this company, and as it turned out, I was right. Within a year and a half, I was promoted to regional sales manager with a three-state territory. Eighteen months later, I was offered another promotion to division sales manager, responsible for the entire Midwest newsstand sales. I was in charge of hiring, training, and sales development. I had several sales managers reporting to me.

The ultimate prize in the world of publishing is New York City. As a result of hard work and a lot of luck, I was promoted to the corporate office smack dab in the "mid" part of midtown Manhattan: Madison Avenue and 45th Street. Five short years, three promotions, and now the corporate office! With the title of territory sales director, I had the top of the corporate ladder within sight. I was successful. I had a prestigious business card, a glamorous midtown address, a nice house in the 'burbs, and a solid future. Life was good.

During my climb up the corporate ladder, I also became more and more involved in my Christian faith. After making a solid run at the Party Animal Hall of Fame during the late '70s and early '80s, I recommitted my life to Jesus Christ at a John Guest Crusade in the late '80s. As my career grew, so did my faith.

I finally reached a point in my life where I knew I needed to serve God in a different way. I had a career, but I felt I needed a vocation. As my wife and I prayed together each morning, I felt God tugging at my heart and soul. I became more and more disillusioned with corporate life, and I felt I needed to change—but how and to what end? I was clueless as to what I should do or how I could leave my career in publishing.

Everything changed one morning in a Detroit hotel room. Preparing for my day of sales calls, I knelt by the side of the bed and prayed. I asked God to reveal to me what he wanted me to do; what change he wanted me to make in my life. I asked God to make his plan obvious and to give me strength to follow that plan. I ended my prayer and waited.

Nothing happened. No angelic hosts of heavenly messengers. No trumpets. No voices. Nothing. Nada. Zilch.

I returned home that evening to a stack of bills and a letter. The letter was addressed to me but was in my own handwriting. Months earlier, in a Bible study, we had concluded the evening by writing letters to ourselves from God. I had completely forgotten about the exercise.

> Dear John,
>
> As I love you, I need you to love others. There are so many needs in my world, and I desperately need your help to fulfill my will on earth.
>
> Please help clothe my naked. Please help feed my hungry. Please help house my homeless.
>
> You have so many gifts. Please continue to encourage others and keep up your sense of humor.
>
> Love,
>
> Your Heavenly Father

When I read that letter, I knew instantly that God wanted me to pursue full-time ordained ministry. The note did not say that. But I felt that my prayer earlier that day in a Detroit hotel room had allowed God to pull at my heart, soul, and mind and align my will with his will. At that moment I had a true sense of God's call to become a pastor.

I shared my feelings with my wife. She had sensed the same thing for me. I tried finding someone to tell me I was nuts. No one would. But then the kicker—I needed to tell my parents that I was leaving a lucrative marketing position with the largest privately held publishing company in the country. I was going from success to the unknown. All I had was a sense of God's call and the clothes on my back. I knew what my dad would say. I knew he would have me make my list of pluses and minuses. I knew he would tell me I needed to be practical. I knew he would tell me to be reasonable and to think of my future and my responsibilities.

Instead, with tears running down all our cheeks, my father looked at me and said, "I know." He blessed my decision and told me not to worry. He told me God would take care of me. He knew that God would give me the faith necessary to fulfill his call.

He was right.

I applied to Yale Divinity School and began the plans to sell our house and use the proceeds to help pay for three years of graduate studies. I studied harder than I had ever studied, and I made it through the rigorous ordination process. My mother died the year I entered seminary. My father died my final year of seminary. School was demanding. Finances were impossible. But God's call was obvious, and finally I was ordained into the United Methodist Church.

Change was not easy for me. It involved great sacrifice. But in the midst of the sacrifice and challenge, I find peace in these words from 2 Timothy:

"So do not be ashamed to testify about our Lord, or ashamed of me his prisoner. But join with me in suffering for the gospel, by the power of God, who has saved us and called us to a holy life— not because of anything we have done but because of his own purpose and grace. This grace was given us in Christ Jesus before the beginning of time" (2 Timothy 1:8-9).

I once thought success was measured through the accumulation of stuff. I now realize success is measured by one's investment into the lives of other people.

John R. Gerlach is an ordained elder in the United Methodist Church and serves the congregation of The United Methodist Church, Branford CT. He received a Masters of Divinity degree in 1996 from Yale Divinity School. He has been married to his lovely wife Joan for 27 years and they have two beautiful children, Bekah, age 12 and A.J. age 8. John entered the ministry after 13 years in the Publishing business having worked most recently with Conde Nast Publications as a Territory Sales Director.

THE SECRET TO BEING HEARD
RANDALL L. FRAME

When I was a young man, I had an opinion on pretty much every issue or topic that I knew anything about. And I felt that it was my duty to express my opinions as often and as forcefully as possible. After all, I did not want the world to be deprived, and I felt that in some way it would be deprived were I to withhold my views. This was especially the case since, as far as I could determine, my opinion on whatever subject was being discussed was, more often than not, the correct one.

My first job out of graduate school was as a news reporter for *Christianity Today* magazine. I drew many interesting assignments, including attending the meetings of major Christian denominations at which delegates would debate controversial issues facing the church, sometimes into the wee hours of the morning. Some of these delegates, like me, felt an obligation at every opportunity to let everyone know what they thought about every single issue.

I will never forget sitting in on a meeting of delegates near the beginning of the annual gathering of the Presbyterian Church USA, some time in the late 1980s. The chief officer of the denomination was giving delegates—particularly the rookies—some advice on convention floor etiquette, or debate decorum. He told them they would have many opportunities over the next few days to rise and speak for or against some issue or policy. He went on to say something along the following lines:

"Everyone should take the opportunity to rise and speak at least once. That way people will know who you are, and many will remember you when you get up to speak a second time. If the second time you speak, you say something interesting or helpful—perhaps even profound—people will make note of it and will look forward to hearing from you a third time. Again, if you have something good to say, they will listen intently—maybe even take notes—when you speak a fourth time and perhaps even a fifth. But that's where you need to draw the line. Because after about five times, no matter how eloquent your words or how logical or profound your arguments, people will start to ignore you. Remember that this convention is not about you. It's about everyone getting an opportunity to be heard. So no matter how smart you are, the smartest thing to do is to be kind and considerate of others."

Since that time, in various employment settings, I've been in a number of meetings where I've noticed people arguing why we should do this thing or that thing, sometimes talking *at* each other instead of *with* one another. Often there is someone in the room who's spent the entire time listening instead of talking. Inevitably, during a break in the action, someone notices and says something like, "Leslie, you haven't said a word this whole time. What do you think?"

And in that moment, Leslie morphs into E.F. Hutton. The whole world stops to hear what Leslie is about to say. Because Leslie has learned that opinions register their greatest influence not when they are foisted upon others but rather when people ask for them and, by doing so, surrender themselves, thus becoming a completely captive audience.

I have gotten much better at picking my battles, choosing my spots. To be sure, I'm not always as much like Leslie as I would like to be. But I'm a whole lot more like Leslie than I used to be. I'm better for it, and so are my opinions now that I'm not the only one listening to them.

Randall L. Frame is executive director of marketing and communications at Eastern University's Palmer Theological Seminary. His writings include ten books and three feature-length screenplays. His 2004 essay, "Fixing Haiti," won a third-place prize in the Templeton Foundation's "Power of Purpose" essay competition in which there were nearly four thousand entries from ninety-seven countries.

FIXING WHAT IS BROKEN
SETH BARNES

The saying, "If you have a hammer in your hand, everything looks like a nail" was true for me. I had seen enough poverty to want to do something about it. As an economics major at Wheaton College, the hammer in my hand was a passion for social justice issues. Tony Campolo had riled me up, and I believed I could make a difference.

Cambodia's tragedy known as the "killing fields" was the greatest social justice cause of my generation. When the call went out to help the hundreds of thousands of Khmer refugees pouring into Thailand, I was among the first to enlist. It didn't matter that I was only twenty-one and leaving behind a woman I'd marry in less than a year: something had to be done.

The refugees we served in the Prasat refugee camp needed so much, but the first things they needed were food and shelter. We helped put them back on their feet economically by setting them up in business as pig and chicken farmers. After that experience, I returned to graduate from college and then headed off to Indonesia and then the Dominican Republic to start microenterprise organizations that would contextualize those same economic development principles. It wasn't a lack of success that caused me to begin to question what

119

I was doing. The organizations I helped start became fabulously successful, creating thousands of jobs for the poor by lending money to small businesses. But I began to ask, *After these people have grown their companies and created new jobs, so what? Was this God's point, or is there more?*

Business school gave me no further clues, but a season of failure that followed it did. When working harder and smarter didn't seem to put much of a dent in the world's pain, I came to the end of myself and my own resources. My job didn't work, my marriage wasn't great, and my religion was bone weary. But in that place of bankruptcy, God showed up. He crashed through my self-sufficiency with a declaration of love and began to lay waste to my concept of what poor people really need—indeed, what all of us need.

My wife, Karen, was pregnant with our fifth child, and the only insurance we had was Medicare. I needed more than just another dollar; I needed hope in the worst way. And God showed me that he cared enough to speak to me and to make our relationship—which I always assumed to be personal—something that I would be prepared to die for.

The experience took a couple of years to work its way through me, but it changed everything. It didn't just change my mind; it changed me at my core—it changed my identity and purpose. I realized from the inside out that Jesus didn't come to give us a better social justice program. I began to understand what he meant when he declared he'd come to set the captives free—free from lies, free from stale religion, and free from anything less than a dynamic personal relationship with him.

I saw that the name of Jesus really does have power. I experienced the reality of prayer—its power to connect man to God's presence, voice, and direction. That connection is the answer to every other social justice issue of life. Salvation is not an afterthought in meeting the world's needs; it's the starting place. Every orphan needs a mother's love, and every refugee needs a home, but without Jesus at the center, the world's social programs are hollow.

Years later when I was leading a team of nine hundred young people to bring an ethic of abstinence to the most HIV-infected country in the world, God brought me up short and reminded me of what he'd shown me years earlier: *Woe to me if I don't preach the gospel.* We were partnering with a governmental organization, and we had been told to not share our faith as we taught in schools around the country. But abstinence by itself, un-tethered to Jesus and his Gospel of hope, is only half the story. To be completely whole, these people needed to learn about Jesus.

I used to think we could solve the world's problems by rolling up our sleeves and working hard to fix whatever is broken. I still believe in working hard and getting my hands dirty, but our work is in vain if we fail to share the love of Jesus and his Gospel.

Seth Barnes is the executive director of Adventures in Missions (AIM), an interdenominational missions organization that focuses on discipleship. Since he founded the organization in 1989, AIM has taken more than eighty thousand people into the mission field, some for as short as a week and others for as long as a year or more. You can follow Seth's blog at sethbarnes.com and learn more about AIM at adventures.org.

MANGO-COLORED NAIL POLISH
ANNIE F. DOWNS

As I type, my fingertips fly from key to key, a blur of bright orange. Mango is my current nail polish color of choice. And while it is somewhat distracting to me (and honestly, anyone else because it is seriously bright!), to see the orange dance across my keyboard speaks of deeper things. It is an outward sign of a healthy heart.

Okay, that might sound a little lame, so let me explain.

All my life, I chewed my fingernails. Big time. I mean—and this is gross—I bit and picked at my nails until they bled. I bit my nails when I was nervous. I bit my nails when I was bored. I bit my nails when I was sad, lonely, busy, scared. It really didn't matter. I bit them down until you could see the tips peeled to deeper levels and the nail bed and quick revealed on each finger. It was ugly.

But so was I.

At least, I thought so. Growing up, I looked in the mirror and saw an ugly face atop an ugly body. My hair was decent, and I was pretty funny, but that didn't atone for the ugliness everywhere else.

The idea of having pretty nails never crossed my mind. Why would I focus on such tiny details when the big picture was hopeless? I figured it was like fixing the light switches in a room to distract the eye from the hideous wallpaper.

In college, the Lord really began to speak to my heart about my identity. The old Annie believed that her outward ugly self canceled out the possibility of beauty on the inside. The new Annie, the one whom God was forming and filling with truth, was learning that inner beauty should be like a well and run over and outward. God began to change the way I thought about myself. How I felt on the inside began to affect how I felt about the outside.

This new Annie had a hard row to hoe: replacing the lies in my head with truth, meditating on Scripture, and choosing to hear God's voice when he called me beautiful, flawless, fearfully and wonderfully made. It took *years* of work and battles (some won, many lost) before I began to wake up in the mornings and see myself the way God sees me.

Just like a flower, I was watering the truth and sitting in the presence of the Son. And in time, I began to bloom. The growth and transformation that happened underground began to surface. As I spent time repairing my inner self, I began to appreciate the view when I looked in a mirror.

I stopped listening to the lies that I was unattractive. I stopped eating whatever I wanted to even if I wasn't hungry. I stopped focusing on the negative attributes of my body. I stopped biting my nails.

I began to read and believe Scripture about how God created me to be exactly who I was, original and unique. I began to exercise and eat in a way that honored God with my body. I began to buy clothes that fit and jewelry that accented my outfits and that actually worked *with* my body instead of hiding what was underneath.

And I began painting my nails.

When gazing at the tiny buds on a growing flower, you notice the growth in the stem, the leaves, and even the roots before you see the bud bloom into a flower. My fingernails, although it seems silly, tell observers about who I am on the inside. Tiny flowers bloom when the entire plant is cultivated.

Biting my nails was a habit I needed to break. It was difficult. Bottles of "stop biting" nail polish piled up in my bathroom drawers. After a bad day, I reverted to biting my nails again and then began the process all over again. In time, the old habit died with the old mindset. And in its place? Beauty.

Winter brings shades of chestnut and mocha. And I hear gray is the color to have in autumn. In spring, I prefer the light pinks, dainty and breezy. And summer? It has become my favorite. Brights. Hot pink. White. Orange. Anything that screams beach! Laughter! Tan! Fruit! Outside!

I changed my mind about my looks. Well, actually, God changed my mind. He took my old mind and made it new. Literally took the ugly and made it beautiful.

And that's what I think when I see these mango fingernails.

Beautiful.

Annie F. Downs tells stories for a living as a freelance writer in Nashville, Tennessee. Flawed but funny, Annie uses her writing to highlight the everyday goodness of a real and present God. You can read more at annieblogs.com. And yes, she is beautiful.

Boys will be boys.

It's the second-deadliest phrase a man's soul can ever allow. Nothing people sum up with *boys will be boys* is ever good for the boy—or for the people around the boy. Sure, it was cute enough when all I was doing was lighting firecrackers in piles of dog waste and running away just before the explosion speckled my little brothers. And it was justification enough for torn clothes, broken bones, or holes in the wall. But *boys will be boys* was also the reason I drove like a maniac; why, when I was in college, I never saw the point in drinking just six beers; why cigars were cool; why I made sure I could handle myself in a fight; why I watched *SportsCenter* three times a day; why boobs had their magical draw; and why I figured a 2.8 was GPA enough for a national merit scholar to earn on his father's tuition dime.

But that's only the second-deadliest phrase. The deadliest is *better safe than sorry.*

Better safe than sorry is how many people make use of the scripture verse about "putting away childish things." It sounds a lot like

127

growing up; because it's so boring, it must be what grownups are supposed to do.

I met my wife after spending five years doing urban ministry in Denver and living like a daredevil for Jesus. And she'd spent an extra year after college in missionary training school and had thought she'd die on the mission field as a daredevil too. We were immediately drawn to each other, but as soon as we committed to each other, we both figured it was time to grow up, and we sold out. We chickened out. We adopted a *better safe than sorry* approach.

Not that we were scared. It was more a matter of not wanting to fail or to cause each other pain. And truth be told, security and safety sounded pretty good to my wife, and having her feel safe and happy made me feel like I was doing the right thing. The grownup thing. The thing you do when you put away childish things.

What happens when a *boys will be boys* person gets older is that he becomes a *guy*. Not a man but a guy. Trucks and guns and hard doctrine and head knowledge and wild-heartedness—a sort of frat boy/meathead mash-up. He has power, but he's a bully with it—selfish and ultimately abusive in the choices he makes.

When a *better safe than sorry* person gets older, he becomes an abdicator. A wimp. He conforms—not to God's call, but to the social pressures that surround him. He becomes the tame nice guy; the ghost in his own home.

The *guy* looks at the *wimp* and says, "No way, I'm gonna let that happen to me." The *wimp* looks at the *guy* and says, "If I have to be a guy to be a man, I'm not interested." And both turn away. And real manhood is left unoccupied.

I used to eat pizza and not work out because the pizza felt like *guy* food, and working out felt vain and prissy. Then I got married and became safe, and pizza felt nostalgic, and not working out felt like one way to retain some control over my world.

And the weight came on. And whether it's weight or some other *guy/wimp* stolen comfort that a person faces, by the time he's about forty, the wheels start wobbling. I crossed a weight a couple of years ago from which less than 3 percent of people ever experience any meaningful or lasting recovery, a weight that translates into a life span that's shortened by twenty to twenty-five years. That means that by the time I'm forty-five, I'll be living on borrowed time.

This is what ambivalence about manhood has gotten me. This is what being unclear about *guy vs. wimp vs. man* has gotten me. It's not a gender thing, by the way—it's just my path to a human truth. What I've learned is that masculine energy is the initiator energy, and feminine energy is the responder energy. Therefore, Jesus is the ultimate in both: the ultimate responder to the Father and the ultimate initiator to humanity.

That's become my role to play too. A man responds to the Father by speaking truth, initiating service, expressing love, showing the way, and facing the realities of life in obedience, even when the decisions are painful. And he understands that he can only fulfill that role in the company of others.

In a couple of months, I will have bariatric surgery so that I can continue to live. I never thought it would come to this.

My *guy* side is embarrassed and feels defeated. My *wimp* side shames me for being so foolish that I'd get to this place.

But my community? My community cheers for me and tells me this is what *men* do.

Pete Gall is a recovering Christian hero whose stories are recorded in two books so far: **My Beautiful Idol** *and* **Learning My Name,** *both published by Zondervan. In addition to writing, he is a brand strategist and occasional church speaker. But his true joy comes from spending time with his wife, a couple small circles of friends in Indianapolis and Nashville, and his two dogs, Abby and Emily. Learn more about Pete at petegall.com.*

LIBERAL *AND* CONSERVATIVE?
GARY MOORE

I'm an investment advisor, finance author, and a man. I do not believe the words *new* and *improved* should be used together. So as I've written repeatedly over the years, I usually change my mind only by running head-on into the wall of Wall Street.

On those rare occasions when I do seek a little guidance, it is usually from one of three sources. They are among those four that John Wesley said shape our worldviews in addition to our *experiences* of hitting the walls of life: Scripture, tradition, and reason. If I wasn't so "manly," I might ask my wife, since studies say women are better investors than men, primarily from being more prudent and patient.

The male-dominated world of finance aspires to operate with a cold and calculated reason. Yet it often seems to have a logic of its own; my experiences are that it isn't always enriching. As evidenced by hedge funds, sub-prime mortgage bonds, and so on, it usually takes a very large mind to create a very large mess. The very largest messes usually occur because some man, convinced of his own omniscience, refused to change his mind until it was far too late.

Then, of course, there are the "evil" minds, as the judge termed the mastermind of Bernie Madoff's ponzi scheme. This ability of the human mind to short-circuit in so many ways is why I like to blend Scripture and tradition to cement my thinking and experiences when making—and particularly reevaluating—critical decisions as I need to change direction.

Scripture has always been very important to me. I grew up in a tiny fundamentalist church. I was always proud that I was one of those "Bible-believing Christians" the world regularly snubs. Because that was important to me, it was also the hardest thing about which to change my thinking. I had been on Wall Street for a decade when I began contemplating seminary (I didn't find the Street to be particularly holy ground). Upon rereading the Bible cover to cover, I realized just how theologically liberal virtually all American Christians, myself included, had become when it comes to money and economics.

Very simply, ancient Israelites lived on less than a current-day equivalent of five hundred dollars per year, and their wealth was in sheep and goats. Even the Bible indicates that Jesus hoped for "a more abundant life" for us than that; perhaps not as materialistically affluent as we are but still more affluent than the ancients enjoyed. That makes progressive economic thought—hopefully guided by the Holy Spirit—probable, if not inevitable. Consider the subject of earning interest on our certificates of deposit, EE bonds, and mutual funds, as C.S. Lewis did in *Mere Christianity*:

"There is one bit of advice to us by the ancient heathen Greeks, and by the Jews of the Old Testament and by the great Christian teachers of the Middle Ages, which the modern economic system has completely disobeyed. All these people told us not to lend money at interest; and lending at interest—what we call investment—is the basis of our whole system. . . . It does not necessarily follow that we are wrong. That is where we need the Christian economist. But I should not have been honest if I had not told you that three great civilizations had agreed in condemning the very thing on which we have based our whole life."

In essence, Lewis was saying that for most of us, religious tradition has superseded Scripture as the basis of our thinking about interest. Only a few old order Amish and Islam continue to shun the earning of interest as they remain People of the Book economically. My later study of economic and church history suggests earning interest was legitimated around the Protestant Reformation. I therefore believe earning and paying interest—even investing itself as we know it—is compatible with traditional Christianity, if not biblical Christianity.

However, biblical principles on the matter still cause me to take a conservative approach. I've always borrowed far less than realtors assure me I could on a mortgage. I've had very little consumer debt over the decades and have only borrowed modestly for the most productive ventures. More importantly, I've generally avoided the pitfalls of junk bond-type investments that require corporations and homeowners to pay the very highest interest. And I began changing my mind about the prospects for the American economy as the new century arrived with total

American debt as a percentage of national income exceeding Great Depression levels.

In other words, over the decades my thoughts about my life as a Christian have changed. Knowing I'm an economic liberal, despite still being rather theologically and socially conservative, has caused me to be more graceful to those who are liberal in other realms of life.

Being honest with myself has been spiritually enriching as I do not need to do theological gymnastics and/or compartmentalize my life as an investment advisor from my beliefs. And that has been an enriching change, both spiritually and financially.

Gary Moore is an investment advisor and the founder of the Financial Seminary, a nonprofit ministry formed to build bridges between the financial and moral communities. His views and writings have appeared in **Forbes, Business Week, Money,** *and* **Christianity Today.** *Learn more about Gary and the Financial Seminary at financialseminary.org/index.php.*

GIVING UP ON CERTAINTY
KARL GIBERSON

"The pursuit of truth will set you free, even if you never catch up with it."
-Clarence Darrow

I used to think that certainty mattered in life. Now I don't.

I was a pretty normal Christian kid when I headed off to college. I had been raised in a conservative evangelical parsonage, and as a budding intellectual, I was into Christian apologetics. It was important to me to be able to prove that my faith was completely true.

I had various arguments at my disposal: fulfilled prophecy showed that God must have written the Bible; problems with evolution showed that creation was true; our sense of morality demanded that there be both a moral law and a lawgiver. Other world religions had serious theological and ethical problems; and gays and secular humanists were obviously following the devil.

All this combined to create a powerful conviction in the deepest part of my soul that I could have 100 percent confidence that my beliefs were *right* and that those with different beliefs were *wrong*.

In my college years, this certainty evaporated. By studying science, I learned that my belief in young-earth creationism was about as credible as my earlier belief in Santa Claus; I learned that the biblical texts were complex, culturally conditioned, and even contradictory. I came to understand that the Bible was not one book written by God but a collection of books written by inspired but fallible humans. And some of the so-called prophecies in the Bible were nothing of the sort, having been written centuries after the events they were supposedly foretelling. I met people from other religions and discovered they were not following Satan. I discovered that morality was far too complicated to be based on a set of laws. But the ultimate jolt to my system was probably when my best friend—whom I had taken a Bible course with—announced that he was gay and then went on to become a minister in a gay church.

Needless to say, these developments laid waste to whatever certainty I had about my faith when I arrived at college. I didn't know what to think.

Like most fundamentalists, I came to college believing that the Bible was either completely accurate in all details, or it was useless as a foundation for faith. But it turns out this isn't true. In fact, I became convinced that certainty was not only an impossible goal, but it was overrated in terms of its importance and even dangerous in terms of its effects because it makes you intolerant.

Absolute certainty is merely something we *want*. We don't *need* it, and we function quite well without it in almost every part of our lives. Think about visiting the mechanic. He tells you to spend $1800 to replace your transmission. Do you demand absolute certainty before you do this? What about your doctor, who tells you that you have a problem with an internal organ and recommends that you let a surgeon cut you open and take it out? Do you demand absolute certainty before you agree to this? On the highway, do you have absolute certainty the oncoming cars will stay on their side of the road?

Every day we make decisions, large and small, based on things that are merely *probable* and never certain. And we function just fine.

I no longer have certainty in my beliefs. I no longer even look for certainty, since I know, with certainty (go figure!), that it cannot be found. What I have now is *faith*—faith that God exists and loves me, faith that this God was revealed in Jesus, faith that I need to love others and will find meaning in doing so. And I have *hope*—hope that heaven is real and that my faith is based on truth. I also have *charity* in the form of tolerance and intellectual humility. Because I know I might be wrong, I can no longer wag my finger at those who think differently and condemn them to hell.

And it seems okay. The dogmatic uniform I once wore no longer fits; and I don't really know how to describe what I am wearing now. But that seems okay too.

Karl Giberson is a physicist and scholar who teaches at Eastern Nazarene College and is an internationally known voice in the creation-evolution debate. He has written several books including **Species of Origins: America's Search for a Creation Story,** *which has been used as a textbook and is considered one of the most balanced treatments of the creation-evolution controversy ever published. His most recent book is* **Saving Darwin: How to Be a Christian and Believe in Evolution** *(HarperOne). Learn more about him at karlgiberson.com.*

I used to think I knew it all.

I should have known better.

But I didn't. In fact, as a hotshot journalist back in the mid-seventies working for what was then the largest evening newspaper in America, I was so distrustful of anyone who professed to be telling the truth that I took it as a personal challenge to prove them wrong.

Pride and arrogance, are, of course, what I was filled with. But I claimed it was journalistic integrity. I told people I was paid to be skeptical. But it wasn't skepticism. That had long since slipped into cynicism.

I worked as an investigative reporter for the *Detroit News* in the 1970s. I traveled so much and covered so many big stories that the newspaper actually took out full-page ads in a newspaper trade publication touting me as "one of America's best-traveled reporters."

Today, as I look at that long-ago ad, I just chuckle. The accompanying photo showed me giving my best skeptical, raised-eyebrow stare and wearing my trademark tan trench coat.

But I was the first to buy my own hype, and in a way, you can't blame me. From mayors to presidents and with every shade of politician in between, I found them all to be spin masters at best, hypocritical liars and scoundrels at the worst. I knew this firsthand. My beat was crime and corruption, and just like burned-out cops sometimes tend to think everyone is a bad guy, I thought those who shouted truth the loudest were usually the most deceptive.

So when I received a letter from a reader one day, it was perfectly in my role as a self-appointed truth detector that I reacted as impulsively as I did.

I wish I remembered the date. More importantly, I wish I remembered who the author of the letter was, for it changed my life.

The letter was from a woman and was handwritten in a meticulous cursive. It was a reaction to some story I had written, no doubt something dealing with crime or the mob or the Mafia. I just don't remember. But it concluded with a Bible verse and, I think, a promise to pray for whatever wretched person or circumstance I was writing about.

I don't recall the verse. I just recall my reaction.

I reached for one of those big red marking pencils that editors used to mark up copy, and I scrawled across it a short message: *I am returning this letter to you as I'm sure you'd want to know some idiot fool is signing your name to letters they're sending newspaper reporters.*

I distinctly remembering showing this to a couple of other reporters who sat near me in the city room. They laughed. I felt so witty as I sealed it in a *Detroit News* envelope and sent it back to the writer.

I then forgot about it until a week later, when my phone rang.

"News...Wendland," I answered in a voice I hoped sounded gruff and tough.

It was the woman who had written me the letter. She introduced herself.

"I just wanted to tell you that it was really me who sent the letter you returned," she said. She sounded elderly. And very polite.

I didn't know what to say. I think my face turned red.

"And I wanted to apologize if there was something I wrote that offended you," she continued. "I just read your story, and I wanted to somehow respond. So I wrote you. What did I write that you took exception to?"

I was convinced she knew. She was trying to set me off guard, I figured. So I turned my momentary discomfort into anger. "It was the Bible verse," I said. "What does that have to do with anything? Why would anyone put such gibberish down and send it to a stranger?"

She apologized again. "I'm so sorry. I didn't mean to upset you. But may I ask, why? Do you know the Bible? Have you ever read it?"

"Of course," I responded. I'm sure I had picked up a Bible somewhere along the line. In a hotel room somewhere, late at night, bored, finding a Gideon Bible in a nightstand. King James English. And I knew I had read the Bible, or some of it, in a comparative literature class in college.

"Just because you believe some ancient book written in an archaic language has relevance in your life, you shouldn't assume that others believe it. It's your truth, lady, not mine. Not any thinking person's. Thanks for the call but please, next time you need to share, spare me."

I hung up. I was steaming inside. Livid. I looked around the newsroom. No one had noticed. I got up, went over to the water fountain, came back to my desk, and half expected her to call back. She didn't. But my emotions were still churning. Why? Why was I reacting so emotionally?

I felt a tad guilty about being so rude to her. She was somebody's grandmother, for crying out loud. She had been nothing but polite. But I was raging inside. Eventually, I calmed down. Then it hit me. If she had pressed me, asked me how much I had read the Bible, or if I knew any verses or could point out any errors or problems, I would have been clueless.

She would have known I was ignorant about the Bible. I didn't know it all. And she would have had me cold if she had pressed. So over the next hour or so, I made a vow. I'd be ready the next time. If she called back or if, down the road, I would be similarly confronted, I needed to be armed with some facts. I'd investigate the Bible just like I investigated the mob. I'd take it apart. Piece of cake.

It didn't happen all at once. My first study was done at a local church. I spotted a notice somewhere that they were doing a twelve-week survey of the Old Testament. Great, I figured. One night a week for three months. That should do it. I'd be an expert.

Something unexpected happened. I got hooked right at the start. It was really interesting. *Sweeping* was the word I remember using, describing the narrative. After that Old Testament survey, there was, naturally, a twelve-week survey of the New Testament. I'd really be an expert then, I figured as I signed up for it too.

Three things convinced me that the Bible was the most reliable book I have ever read.

The historical record—what we reporters call the paper trail. Documents. I found the Bible—written over a span of 1,500 years by more than forty different authors on three continents—to be simply amazing in its narrative consistency. The versions we have now are true to the original manuscripts, of which we have so much historical evidence that the conflicts or uncertainties would fill only a page or so, none dealing with substantive doctrinal matters.

I also took note of the eyewitness testimony. Of the closest followers of Christ, all died horrible deaths that could have been avoided if they had simply renounced their faith. None did. People don't die for a lie. The Bible had more witness statements than I'd ever need to write a news story.

Finally, my personal observation of Christians had a huge impact on me as my twelve-week surveys moved to studies on individual books of the Bible and I began regularly attending church. Over time, I saw firsthand many people whose lives were dramatically, totally changed. In 1982, in my living room, I became one of them. A believer. First in Jesus Christ, and then in the amazing book that tells the story of mankind's need of a Savior.

That was more than a quarter century ago.

Today, I stand as proof positive that God has a sense of humor. Today, I'm a pastor. A Bible teacher. I read the Bible through each year. I read different translations, commentaries, concordances, devotionals, and a library of study material and software that have become some of my most valued possessions.

How come?

Because I picked up the Bible and started to investigate.

I also found I wasn't the only person who came to faith from pride and arrogance. Many, many others, others much more gifted than me, undertook similar quests and have come away similarly changed over the years.

For me, it all started with a letter from a very nice woman whose faith led not just to a change of mind for a cynical reporter but, truly, to a change of heart.

Mike Wendland, known in his industry as "PC Mike," is a veteran broadcast and print reporter and columnist and has been doing special PC Mike tech segments for NBC-TV affiliates since 1994. Mike has also been the technology columnist for the **Detroit Free Press,** *and his columns and stories have appeared in hundreds of newspapers across the U.S., including* **The New York Times** *and* **USA Today.** *He also is pastor and part of the teaching team of Woods Church. You can follow Mike at pcmike.com.*

THAT WAS THE PLAN
HEATHER KULAGA

Before the rock and roll band, I thought I knew how my life would go. I had a very specific plan: College. Marriage. A teaching career. Motherhood.

And music mixed in there too. Maybe playing the piano in the traditional service at church and giving private music lessons at home. Or just quietly humming a tune to myself as I fixed supper, waiting for my husband to walk in the door at the end of a long day.

I grew up in church—I played there, sang there, prayed there, and even slept there a few times. My friends were church friends. I went to a private Christian college and married another pastor's kid like myself.

When I was young, my mother stayed home, washed our clothes, mended our socks, kissed us, fed us, and read us bedtime stories. The women at my church did the same with their children, chatting in kitchens while their husbands served on boards and ate their potluck dinners. I loved and admired these women and figured I would be just like them when I grew up. That was the plan.

Before the rock band.

Four children and many traditional services after getting married, I started to realize how small my world was. Neat. Compact. Easy to manage. I have never been one to leave well enough alone. It all began a few years ago when our family moved away from my childhood church and my piano was put into temporary storage. The only instrument I had was my grandma's old guitar. I picked it up, took some lessons, and learned to play. By the time my piano emerged from the storage facility, I had figured out that our new church didn't need another pianist.

What they really needed was a bass player.

So I studied and practiced and listened to music. I joined the church band, started an electric bass duo, and played in coffee shops. I played my bass at other churches and for banquets, at art shows and nursing homes. I made new musical friends and began learning about all kinds of music—music that was way different from anything I'd ever heard growing up.

One day I was invited to an audition. I sat in the middle of a room of accomplished, seasoned musicians and listened to them jam. My hands were trembling. I had no idea what to do. There was no music written down. No notes, certainly no hymnal. All that I saw and heard was freedom, joy, and sharing. When I stepped into that music, I stepped out of all my previous plans.

Ten years ago I had hardly even held a guitar in my hand and I thought the new contemporary service was too loud.

Now, sixteen years after quitting my job as a first-grade teacher to stay home full time and raise a family, I am just returning from a weekend gig with the world-fusion rock band I joined that night. Twenty years into my carefully laid life plans, I find myself recovering from a four a.m. bedtime at a strange hotel many miles away from home.

It's a good thing the pastor's kid I married is a patient man.

Most nights I fall into bed way later than the rest of the family. I'm working with new friends, some of whom never darken a church door. I know how to recognize the smell of marijuana now and how not to get hugged by an alcohol-soaked fan.

I am more likely to be practicing my bass, playing a gig, or running off to a rehearsal than to be fixing a home-cooked supper for my husband.

What happened to the plan?

I loved the safety and warmth of my little family at home. But as my children grew, I realized that their metamorphosis was a natural and beautiful thing. And that changing is what living is all about. So I decided to keep growing right along with them. Letting go of hand-me-downs when they no longer fit, facing the unknown, falling down and making a few messes, just like they do.

I still love my husband, contribute to potluck dinners, do laundry, and read bedtime stories. And I still make plans. I just make sure to leave room for them to grow.

Heather Kulaga is a musician, wife, and mother of four children living in Webberville, Michigan. She is currently the bassist for Thom Jayne and the Nomads, a world-fusion rock band. Listen to samples of their music, order their CDs, or check out their booking information at thomjayneandthenomads.com.

LEAVING SUCCESS FOR SIGNIFICANCE
LLOYD REEB

I used to think life was simple—you get the best grades so you can get into the best school so you can get the best job so you can accumulate the most toys so you can retire as early as possible. I spent the first half of my life doing just that. Today, at age forty-seven, I have seen that story play out in my own life and in the lives of hundreds of successful people whom I have coached through midlife and have concluded this: all our winning has cost us too much.

It turns out life's not that simple—it's actually simpler. In fact, simpler is better. It boils down to the simple premise Jesus taught: it's better to give than to get. A generation of successful baby boomers is now looking for simpler and more meaningful lives. They want their lives to count for something more, something eternal. The legacy they want to leave? Lives of significance.

That's exactly what I did when I found myself in my early thirties having been successful at real estate development and longing to invest my life in something that wouldn't be torn down in a hundred years. I made a midlife transition to reorient my life toward things I consider significant. I no longer have that sick feeling in my stomach of being trapped in a life of busyness, pursuing things that will not last at the expense of things I value more.

It seems strange to me that I work just as hard as before but somehow know I am free of the rat race. I feel very little stress, at least compared to the gut-wrenching stress I experienced in my first half of life as a real estate developer.

I feel privileged that early in life I could push the pause button and look back on the lessons and accomplishments of the first half, reflect on what will really matter in the long run, and then redirect my life for the second half. Without millions of dollars in the bank, it took creativity and intentionality to discover a way to pursue significance.

You have the same opportunity today, and you don't have to wait until you are in the middle of your life and affluent before you can pursue your life calling. You can instead integrate significance into your life now, and in the process find more meaning and purpose—perhaps even adventure. I see a growing number of young, talented Christian marketplace leaders charting a different course, choosing to swim upstream in our culture, away from a focus on the temporary toward a focus on the eternal, simplifying their lives so they can focus on the things that really matter.

I didn't sell my business or quit my job. Instead I redefined success, reallocated my energies, and reprioritized my family's spending. I cut the time I spent doing business and found a niche where I could use my unique gifts to meet the deepest needs of others. As a result, over the past decade my wife, Linda, and I have had more time to spend with our three kids as they have grown, time to spend together playing tennis and sailing. I have enjoyed getting back in shape physically and building a few close friendships. By allocating part of my week to ministry, I've had the thrill of being a part of many men and women's spiritual journeys as they pursue God and explore their personal faith. I feel blessed to have the freedom to invest a good part of my life in things that I believe will have eternal significance.

And you know the interesting thing? What makes this possible in my life is not that I am rich, smart, or lucky. What has made my life today so dramatically different from the lives of the typical forty-something executives who live and work in my community has been choices, not chance. It's about options, not affluence. It's more about availability than ability. It's not downplaying the thrill and value of success. Instead, it's about building off of your success and transforming it into significance.

Get clear, get free, and get going!

Lloyd Reeb is the primary spokesperson for the Halftime organization (halftime. org), helping successful people pursue significance. He is the author of **From Success to Significance** *and* **The Second Half: Real stories. Real adventure. Real significance.**

FROM RELIGIOUS TO SPIRITUAL
ACE COLLINS

When I was in my late twenties I had a great respect for all denominations. After all, I had grown up in a Lutheran community, my best friend was a Methodist, and another close friend was a Catholic. I had four cousins who were Church of Christ ministers, my favorite pastor was Presbyterian, and one of my business associates was Pentecostal. Yet in spite of my deep respect and admiration for these people and their views on faith, I was a Baptist, and I knew we had it right. In other words, I was sure that I was a member of the best-centered and most spiritual denomination.

My attitude was one born of a family with a deep history in the Baptist church. My grandfather was a Baptist preacher, my great-grandparents and their parents and all my mother's family for generations had been Baptists. I didn't go so far as to condemn anyone because they sprinkled at baptisms while we "held them under until they bubbled," yet I did feel that if others would just visit our services, listen to a few sermons, and learn all the words to "Victory In Jesus" and "Just As I Am," then they would be much more fulfilled as Christians.

Up until the age of thirty I was a Baptist first and a Christian second. When I began writing for World Missionary Evangelism

(WME), a nonprofit, nondenominational Christian organization headquartered in Dallas, Texas, I finally began to wake up. WME worked in a half dozen different countries all around the globe. They didn't need to form a committee to decide what action to take. Their people fed the hungry, clothed the naked, built and ran children's homes for orphans, drilled water wells for the thirsty, and set up medical clinics for the sick.

A decade ago in Kenya, WME drilled a well in a Maasai tribal area. As water gushed from the ground, an elderly warrior walked over to the director of the organization and asked this question: "Did your God do this?" WME's director, John Cathcart, paused for a moment, smiled, and assured him this was a Christian work. At that moment the man gave his heart to the Lord. After they had prayed, did John ask the African to give up three of his four wives to conform to a Western view of marriage? Did John present the old warrior with a list of rules to keep that most American churches required at the time? No. He simply asked him to follow Christ. It was that simple.

Before working with WME, I had never thought about being religious, but that is really what I had become. I was a man whose faith was based upon traditions and convictions. Some of those convictions may have come from the Bible, but that's not really why I followed them. I inherited them from my Baptist ancestors. In fact, I saw Jesus as a Baptist. In that way, I had become a modern-day Pharisee. I felt that to be completely right, you had to do things my way.

Over the years I have been exposed to a plethora of people and organizations that worked well outside the spheres of traditional Christian framework. They are not concerned with adhering to old practices or rules; instead they are strictly focused on living out Christ's teachings. They seek out those in need, meet those needs, and live their faith through their actions.

As I have grown older I feel that maybe men like U2's Bono have it right. The rock star is deeply spiritual, and he emulates Christ in actions but leaves the sermons to someone else. Bono seems more interested in studying the Bible than he is on making sure everyone else sees his interpretation of those words as the best way to faith.

When I am now asked, "What religion are you?" I don't make the mistake of my youth. I don't say "Baptist." Instead I say "Christian." I am still active in my local Baptist church, but today I am sure I will be measured not by my church's doctrine or my ability to be religious but by the way I employ my convictions to make this world better for the least of these. My young view of faith could be found in traditions while my mature faith can be found in Matthew 25:35-40, summarized with these words from Jesus: "Whatever you did for the least of these brothers of mine, you did it for me."

Master storyteller Ace Collins is the award-winning author of more than sixty books, including the thriller **Farraday Road,** *the first book in the* **Lije Evans Mysteries** *series. He has appeared on* **NBC Nightly News, Good Morning America, The Today Show, CBS Early Show, Entertainment Tonight,** *and scores of other national and local television shows. A popular radio guest and speaker nationwide, Collins lives and writes in Texas. Learn more about Ace and his 1965 Mustang at: acecollins.com.*

RANDOMIZING RITUALS
LEONARD SWEET

I have changed my mind about so many things so many times that it's hard to know where to begin. Perhaps the biggest mind change that led to a change-my-life moment was the period in my mid-thirties when God knocked me off my high Gutenberg horse, roughed me up a bit, and said, "Sweet, are you going to get a ministry for the world you've got or the world you wish you had?"

Up until that time I was a typical academic, a categorical imperialist about book culture who evaluated every new development in digital technology from the lofty, linear categories of print. Not surprisingly, I found digital culture falling way short, loopy, and fuzzy, and even wrote a never-published critique of electronic culture that echoed Neil Postman's *Amusing Ourselves to Death*. Once I began to understand digital culture by standing under that culture and not privileging print culture, however, a whole new way of seeing the world opened up. This native of a Gutenberg world is still struggling to find his way as an immigrant in a Google world, and I increasingly sit at the feet of Googley natives for the cues and clues as to what is going on out there.

Instead of piling up more examples, however, let me unveil one of my "secrets" that opens my life up to "black swans"—unpredictable, hard-to-see, outlier phenomenon—and forces me to stray from paddocks that quickly become padlocks. A key way I keep creative is to engage in what I call "randomizing rituals" that rout routine in my life.

One of the best compliments you can pay me is, "That's so random!" In Gutenberg culture, a "random existence" was morally destitute, self-indulgent, and ruinously out of control. Puritans especially were fond of decrying the "random existence" of hedonists and other pagans. But randomizing rituals and practices help me escape aging's coffins of conformity. In fact, neuroanatomists who can read the colors of the "brainbow" are now telling us that dreaming requires randomization, since dreams are caused by random brainstem brainstorms, stimulations of the cerebral cortex.

I am not the first to advocate randomizing rituals. Augustine liked to open Paul's epistles at random and one day found a divine light flooding his heart when he did so. Leave it to Methodism's founder, John Wesley, to make a rule out of random, encouraging his itinerants sometimes to read the Bible using the *at-random rule*, stretching their hands randomly into the lucky dip, and then taking what your finger plopped on as a providential passage. In *Either/Or* (1843), Søren Kierkegaard makes the case for crop rotation in life to curb boredom, keep the mental fields fertile and full of nutrients, and face the responsibilities of an ethical existence.

Here are some examples of my randomizing rituals:

1. Instead of picking out a movie to see, I go to the movies under the discipline of seeing the next movie that is showing when I arrive at the ticket counter. Yes, even if that movie is *27 Dresses* (2008).

2. Install the *stumbleupon.com* toolbar.

3. Pick with eyes closed from the magazine racks of *Hudson News*, one periodical for every hour I'm in flight, with the discipline of reading every page (not necessarily every word) of the periodical in that one hour of flight. On a five-hour flight, I've been exposed to five periodicals that I never would pick up any other way.

4. Take make-it-up-as-you-go rides in the car and stop at odd restaurants or coffee shops you never would pick out by natural inclination or interest.

5. Decline the passiveness of coincidence or chance. Admit no coincidences, only "God-incidences," only connections. "As luck would have it, Providence was on my side," to quote the words of Samuel Butler's hero in *Erewhon*.

Icons provide symbolic carriers for profound subjects like randomization, and my icon for these rituals is a book by Stanford computer scientist Donald E. Knuth, who is most known for his classic text *The Art of Computer Programming*. But Knuth has an iconic presence in my life because this lifelong Lutheran has memorialized in book form what he calls the most "scientific reading of the Bible." Using the random sampling method of Bible reading, Knuth personally translated from the Hebrew and

Greek all fifty-nine 3:16 texts, wrote a theological commentary on each, and commissioned fifty-nine of the world's greatest calligraphers to put these texts into visual form. A signed copy of his book *3:16* and a poster with all fifty-nine calligraphers' art hanging in my Drew University office remind me of the change-my-mind creativity that is unleashed by randomizing rituals.

Leonard Sweet is a theologian, author, and futurist. Currently he is the E. Stanley Jones professor of Evangelism at Drew University. His many books include **The Gospel According to Starbucks, The Three Hardest Words in the World to Get Right,** *and* **The Church of the Perfect Storm.** *As a popular speaker, Len has captivated audiences in Hong Kong, Australia, New Zealand, Brazil, South Africa, China, and Iceland. See what he's up to next at leonardsweet.com.*

NO PASSPORTS IN HEAVEN
DAVID C. BRUSH

 180

I once had the Christian thing figured out. It was a very simple and neatly contained system in which everything made perfect sense. In this Christian system there was a B for every A, a two for every one, and a big dividing line with the Bible and Jesus on one side and the world on the other. Every good Christian American was a Republican, every vote was on one issue, and Ted Kennedy was the sworn enemy. No nuance, no room for argument, and no doubt that if Jesus were born today he would be a red-state-loving American.

Like many Americans, I watched dumbfounded as the Twin Towers fell in 2001. I shared with my fellow Americans the atmosphere of shock and confusion that permeated our country in those first few days afterward. Just as the force of the planes exploding into those mighty towers weakened the steel that held them up, so we as a nation were shook to our core as militant Islam brought to bear its interpretation of Allah's judgment on our American dream. Initially there was an outpouring of compassion for the victims and their families. We watched as celebrities on television pleaded for the funds necessary to ensure the well-being of all those affected, and we responded generously.

The secondary response, if you remember or took part, was one of intense patriotism and a fierce nationalism. We were angry. For some, this nationalism turned into an intense hatred for the Muslims who had attacked us. Enraged and unarmed with clear answers to our questions, we proceeded to engage in a war against Al Qaeda and the Taliban in Afghanistan, a war that is still underway as I write this and for which there seems to be no end in sight.

Five and a half years after the Twin Towers fell, the foundation on which I had built my Christian construct finally began to crack, to succumb to the forces of the Holy Spirit, and I began an earnest spiritual quest. Up until then I had wanted to keep my Christian box right where I had it, under my control. As the political conflicts continued around the world, I began questioning the righteousness and validity of our twin wars in Afghanistan and Iraq. I had friends who had seen combat or were still in harm's way. I struggled with doubt because I felt that not supporting the conflicts would somehow dishonor their brave service to our country.

I had become an avid listener of conservative talk radio in my daily commutes between home and work. If you are not familiar with conservative talk radio in the United States, it is a genre that is almost entirely fueled by the draping over and enshrouding of the cross of Christ with a veil of patriotic nationalism. Many churches today still prominently display the American flag in their sanctuaries, evidence of the common acceptance of this dualistic notion of a modern Christian empire and a testament to the depth to which this myth has permeated the body of Christ in America. An attack on America, according to this philosophy, is an attack on God's people, and anyone who dares to oppose the wisdom of conservative politics, preemptive war, and free-market economics is a godless communist.

How did I change my mind? At first it was through small changes in my sources of information—by listening to a new podcast, for instance, or by reading news sources other than Fox News and the *Washington Times*. The linchpin linking my different ideologies broke apart as I read through authors like John Howard Yoder and Greg Boyd. It became increasingly clear to me that the way I had idolatrously linked together my American citizenship and my citizenship in the kingdom of God was an unholy and dualistic union. I began to see and accept the hurt of the Afghan people not only at the hands of the Taliban and Al Qaeda but also at the hands of my own country. The Afghans and Iraqis were no longer those people over there who had warred against God's people, but they were in some cases my own brothers and sisters in Christ.

I have changed in that God has totally blown apart my system for appropriating his good will for my own blessing. I have changed in that the Holy Spirit has given me eyes to see the humanity in everyone and the worthlessness of no one. I have changed in my perspective on nationalism in that I am first and foremost a child of the King, and my citizenship transcends the kingdoms and kings of this world. I have changed in that I am continually humbled by and amazed at the power of a submitted and contrite heart in the hands of a loving God and in communion with the Holy Spirit.

It is from this changed place of kingdom citizenship and humbled perspective that I have begun to see that there is only one allegiance that matters to me, and that is to my Lord—the Lord of all creation. He is the Lord of the American and the Afghan, of the Chinese and the Iraqi, and the Christian and the Muslim.

All will appear at the throne of judgment, and unless I missed a verse, I don't think they are screening passports for that event.

David C. Brush is a graduate student at Fuller Seminary, where he is studying missional church leadership. He currently lives in Gardner, Kansas, with his wife and two children and is a member of Trinity Family Church of the Nazarene.

EQUATING CERTAINTY WITH FAITH
DANIEL CHESNEY

Like many people who grew up in church, the foundation for my faith came from my parents. When I was four years old my father had a brain aneurism and died shortly after. However, I was young and still had my mother to fall back on. She became the foundation through which I could build an understanding of God. She modeled grace and love. Even through the terrible and unexpected loss of my father, she kept her faith and continued to fervently serve God and the church.

Then my mother was diagnosed with leukemia, and my faith began to crumble. She had been a faithful servant of God her whole life: never missed Sunday school, gave generously to the church, and served as president of the church's missions group for twenty years. Yet God had left her all alone with three children. I could handle that, but then on October 29, 2001, she left this world.

I was twelve.

Throughout the Old Testament, we read that when the Israelites disobeyed the covenant law, God cursed them and gave them over to their enemies. Yet when they followed God, they received bless-

175

ings. My mother had lived up to her part of the covenant; why had God not lived up to his?

My faith took a real hit, but my parents had modeled God in such a way that I held on, and like a lot of conservative Christians in crisis, I reverted to fundamentalism. The only way I could believe in God was through rigid obedience. I separated myself from the world and became obsessive about church attendance. Whenever I failed to live up to the standards by which I had built my understanding of God, guilt settled in like an oppressive tyrant.

As time progressed, I added new standards into my fundamentalist portfolio. Right before leaving for college I became an adamant literal seven-day creationist. I had decided you couldn't actually believe in God without holding this view. In my eyes, abandoning a literal view of the first chapters of Genesis removed all authority from the Bible.

But instead of strengthening my foundation of faith, all of these attempts at certainty slowly eroded it. I began to question everything I believed. For example, I explored what a God-centered view of evolution would mean for my faith and was surprised to find that it didn't weaken it. As I studied, I found that in fact it might make my faith stronger.

My creation view was still transitioning when a speaker asked, "What would shatter your faith if it was proven false?" I thought about my belief that God blesses the faithful. Yet losing both of my parents who had been so faithful hadn't really destroyed my faith—it simply had forced me to find a new foundation.

At one time I thought that abandoning a literal view of a seven-day creation would plunge me into atheism, but exploring an alternative view did not erode my faith. I realized faith was a gift from God, not something that I had to build through knowledge. Up until that point, I had spent my whole life creating foundations for God when he never needed them. I thought that I had to *build* a knowledge of God, but he has freely *given* it through his grace.

I used to think questioning my beliefs was wrong but have come to see that when we ask those tough questions, it allows God to reveal himself anew. Thinking through everything I believe and being willing to lose any seemingly critical part of my faith has not decreased my faith but made it stronger.

Daniel Chesney is a Ministry and Theology student at Southern Nazarene University. He has spent his life growing under the guidance and love of Living Word Church of the Nazarene, Houston.

WHY I BELIEVE IN CELIBACY
RICHARD MORGAN A.J. ROMERO

I started out as a Protestant who was going to marry, have his 2.3 children, snip, and that would be the end. Somehow along the way, I ended up a Catholic celibate on the road to priesthood.

I remember the usual things most converts take their time with, or just ignore. Mary. Purgatory. Birth control. Of the three, the last seemed the most personal, and I remember thinking it didn't really matter what certain couples decided to do for themselves because sex is great (so I've heard) and priests just don't want people to have fun if they can't.

As I grew, though, I realized that the Church's stance on contraception makes a great deal of sense—and often, it makes the most sense to the celibate. We have the luxury of being objective in the matter. We don't come home from a hard day at work, eat a good meal, and think, *Hey, I know what would make my night much better. Where's the wife?* We can see sexuality as the beautiful gift it is because we have decided, for the sake of our fellow men (and women), to sacrifice that gift.

Now, obviously there are much better people who have written much more eloquently on the subject (Paul VI and John Paul II come immediately to mind), but a lot of times, Europeans who live in gold houses seem distant from John Q. Layman, who sincerely loves his wife and doesn't necessarily think it's a grand idea to have ten kids. Besides, *Papal Encyclicals* aren't exactly next to *Harry Potter* on the bestseller lists, partly because academic language doesn't make up most everyone's go-to genre, and also because, of all the plots in the universe, many times we're least intrigued by our own. Furthermore, what can a celibate know about sex? Plenty—at least, the parts that have to deal with sharing in the familial, creative bond of the Trinity (three persons, not just two), not to mention the unshakably romantic nature of it: that it is a complete gift of self to the other person.

Contraception says, "Here's most of me, minus the fertility. Enjoy."

Take out the condom, the pill, or the surgery from the equation, and you're saying, "I love you with my entire being. I give myself completely to you, as you are giving yourself completely to me." It's complete intimacy, and it still gives me chills to think about.

Do I think couples who use contraception are going to hell? No, not really. But I do think they are missing out on a great chance for pure intimacy—and it saddens me. As a celibate, I don't want people to miss out on what I have willingly given up.

It took me years to come to see things this way, but through prayer, reading, and simple observation, I have come to understand what I am really sacrificing. It isn't the sex; it's the intimacy.

Richard Morgan A. J. Romero is a graduate of MidAmerica Nazarene University putting his degree in theology to use in the airline industry. A former Benedictine postulant, he plans to enter a mendicant religious order in the near future.

THE GIFT OF DOUBT
J. PAUL PEPPER

Being an ex-fundamentalist is like being an ex-spouse who has come out of an unhealthy and abusive relationship. In my case, it's like being an ex-spouse who came to the realization of such abuse over an extended period of time. I certainly didn't change my mind about it overnight.

My thinking used to look like this: *I've got the answers. I've got the truth. I've got the arguments.* I carried them around like a cell phone in my pocket, neatly tucked away, to be used however and whenever I wished. When my answers were challenged, when my truth collapsed, when my arguments crumbled, I simply strengthened my grip on what I already thought I knew.

Now my standard of thinking looks like this: *Search for the answers. Seek the truth. Consider the arguments.* In fact, it was this very kind of thinking that allowed me to begin questioning fundamentalism at all. It was embracing open-mindedness with a humble and inclusive thought process that allowed me to begin seeing other viewpoints as potentially valid.

It's easy to think that a person who considers all arguments would not be capable of strong faith, nor secure in the belief of anything lasting. On the contrary, my foundation is more secure than ever because it isn't based on the things about which I'm certain but is instead based upon the God with whom I'm in relationship. As Paul Tillich has said, "Doubt does away with belief but leads to faith."

Through many conversations and circumstances, through many interactions and exchanges of ideas, because of relationships and people caring enough to engage me and challenge my words and ways, I began to grasp how my false certainty was perverting the true Christian thought and life I desired with all my heart. God bless these dear souls for their patience and understanding, for seeing that my heart desired God's truth even while my thinking was so far from him.

What I was missing by pretending to be certain was the beauty of the *journey*. Certainty makes the journey unnecessary. If I've already got the answers, there's no point in continuing on the way. Christian certainty talks about walking with God then acts like the process of discovering more of him is a perversion of the Gospel.

If I *know* women don't belong in ministry, I can't walk with them just enough to realize overwhelmingly how called and gifted they are to carry on the work of the Gospel. If I *know* that Scripture is a long series of propositional truths to be interpreted literally, I can't creatively pursue with others what it means to embody the stories of our faith in this current cultural context. If I *know* the book of Revelation was written to foretell in detail the end of our age event by event, I can't imaginatively explore with God's called-out people what it means to live the life of God's future kingdom here and now. If I *know* Jesus came to die simply so I could be forgiven of *my* sins, I can't perceive the beauty of God's fully redemptive purpose for *all* creation. And if I'm enduringly homophobic, I can't listen long enough to hear and take to heart the stories of the marginalized.

For me, to not take this journey to know God, to stay close-minded, to allow my faith to be perverted, to accept the abuse of fundamentalism as the essence of Christian thought and life, is a real and certain tragedy. Now I realize that the power and ability to change my mind, to realize, process, perceive, grow, and mature in turn, is one of the greatest gifts God gives me in seeking more of him. Such empowerment is a core part of what it means to be fully human and truly alive.

J. Paul Pepper serves as the minister of youth at Blue Springs Church of the Nazarene in Blue Springs, Missouri. He attends Nazarene Theological Seminary where he is pursuing a Masters in Divinity. An aspiring writer and theologian, J. Paul also leads worship and teaches piano. He believes strongly in the powers of community and conversation. He and his beautiful wife, Leah, have one crazy awesome cat named Kung Fu Kittybug.

WHY LUCAS LIVED
JONATHAN COLLINS

I grew up in a genuine Christian home. We were the textbook *first to arrive, last to leave* church family with blond heads and black shoes. Be it Sundays, Wednesdays, church camps, or potlucks, I was bound to be found punching my young clock with the church's churchiness. Such an upbringing had me jaded to many of the harsh realities of the world. But no reality is as harsh as enduring the death of a loved one.

Death has an awkward effect on people's words. It can silence the greatest of teachers and have the simpleminded explaining life's deepest mysteries. Either way, when all is said and done, no one actually has an honest idea whether what they are saying is true.

When my close friend died in sixth grade of an enlarged heart, people comforted me with the supposed truth that his heart was "just too big for this world;" heaven needed him more than we did. And I believed them.

When my unborn nephew and his mother died in a car wreck while I was in junior high, they told me both were in heaven, playing together and waiting to greet us on the other side. And I believed them.

When my brother died from a bicycle accident while I was in high school, I was told he had lived a century's worth of adventure in his nineteen years. They said maybe God took him in the small window that his rebellious heart had turned back to true salvation. And I believed them.

Recently I lost the youngest friend I've ever had and am at a complete loss as to why he was taken from this world. Little Lucas—an eleven-month-old, happy towhead of light—died unexpectedly and without cause while napping in his carseat. One could wonder oneself sick with the questions of what happened, and more importantly, why.

Quickly realizing that no such answers exist, I've found myself holding to something stronger than a cozy explanation. I've found my comfort in a better question. For the first time in my life, I've changed my question after an unexpected death from, *Why did they die?* to the more important one of, *Why did they live?*

Though the sting of death is never quickly remedied, this new question brings an honest purpose to my pain. Why did beautiful baby Lucas *live?*

Literally snatched from the abortion table by the bravery and faith of a single, scared-out-of-her-mind mother, Lucas lived.

In a large city with no extended family and little support, Lucas lived.

*Being unable to speak yet helping to grow the maturity
and purpose of his mother,*
Lucas lived.

*Nearly invisible to an uninvolved father but convicting him
to cry out to God in desperation,*
Lucas lived.

*Not yet knowing how to express his emotions but
somehow strengthening the bond of love in my own
marriage,*
Lucas lived.

*Learning loyalty and dependency on his mother while
silently teaching her to do the same with her sister,*
Lucas lived.

*Being faithful to the meaning of his name by bringing light
to every room he entered, Lucas lived.*

In my life, I have been forced to learn the painful reality that everyone I will ever love must someday die, typically without spiritual explanation. Little Lucas has taught me not to search out the reasons loved ones are taken but to embrace the reasons they were given.

Thank you, Lucas, and thank you, God, for involving me in your reason for living.

Jonathan Collins is a writer and speaker for youth and is actively involved in a new church plant. He is also pursuing his Olympic dreams in the world's most challenging athletic endeavor, the decathlon. Jonathan resides in Southern California with his junior high sweetheart wife and their brand new baby boy, Leo.

EPILOGUE

Christians will always be open to mistaken accusations of being unthinking lemmings. After all, we fix our eyes on the unseen eternal, and many people cannot reconcile where intellectual honesty fits into matters of faith.

Jesus told us to seek first his kingdom. We begin to discover his kingdom in scripture and prayer. We discover it in careful thinking on the issues, and in deep reflection on our experiences. We discover it in the time-tested traditions of Christianity, and with wise counsel from other Christians. And like Abraham leaving Ur, the journey rarely seems a straight line to the promise.

The important thing we find in *180* is not the actual decision each of these Christians has come to—there is plenty of room for respectful disagreement in the kingdom—but the model they provide of challenging their deeply held convictions as they continue to seek the kingdom in an evermore faithful way.

This seems an antidote to those who might have grown up in a world where religious fervor was measured by how well each person accepted the faith of his or her spiritual fathers, without the holy curiosity necessary to making the faith of their fathers truly theirs.

And so we leave you with the plea that you do as Christ said—seek the kingdom, regardless of your present spiritual maturity—so that you may more fully live into the abundant life he has promised.